Woodworking
SIMPLIFIED

THE WEEKEND PROJECT BOOK SERIES

Woodworking Simplified, by David & Jeanie Stiles
Garden Projects You Can Build, by David & Jeanie Stiles
Kids' Furniture You Can Build, by David & Jeanie Stiles
Playhouses You Can Build, by David & Jeanie Stiles

A WEEKEND PROJECT BOOK

Woodworking
SIMPLIFIED

Foolproof Carpentry Projects for Beginners

DAVID & JEANIE STILES

WITH ILLUSTRATIONS
BY DAVID STILES

CHAPTERS PUBLISHING LTD., SHELBURNE, VERMONT 05482

Published by Chapters Publishing Ltd.
2031 Shelburne Road
Shelburne, Vermont 05482

Library of Congress Cataloging-in-Publication Data

Stiles, David R.
    Woodworking simplified: foolproof carpentry projects for beginners /
David and Jeanie Stiles; with illustrations by David Stiles
        p.   cm — (The weekend project book series)
    Includes bibliographical references and index.
    ISBN 1-881527-98-0 (softcover)
    1. Woodwork—Amateurs' manuals. 2. Woodwork—Patterns
    3. Woodworking tools.
    I. Stiles, Jeanie. II. Title. III. Series.
    TT185.S74 1996
    684'.08—dc20   95-51859

Printed and bound in Canada by Tri-Graphic Printing Ottawa Ltd.
Ottawa, Ontario

Book design by Eugenie Seidenberg Delaney
Photography by Skip Hine

All designs by the author, unless otherwise noted.

To Jeanie's mother,

Jean Trusty Daniel,

who always hits the nail on the head—

simply the greatest!

ACKNOWLEDGMENTS

We wish to thank Lucy and Vanessa Biery, Jeanne Bockman, and Darcy and Richard Bockman, for allowing us to photograph in their homes, and Danielle Bockman, for being a perfect model even during a heat wave.

We would also like to thank everyone at Chapters Publishing for their enthusiasm and support for this book: Barry Estabrook, our publisher, Sandy Taylor, our editor, Eugenie Delaney, the book designer, Emily Stetson, our copy editor, Alice Lawrence, the managing editor and Melissa Cochran, the editorial assistant.

Once again we were fortunate enough to have Skip Hine photograph our projects. His talent, energy and willingness to work under battlefield conditions resulted in spectacular photographs.

CONTENTS

INTRODUCTION

DAVID'S LOVE OF CARPENTRY began when he was a small boy, watching his father shape a baluster on a wood lathe. David had accidentally broken one on the front hall stairs while sliding down it. He watched with amazement as his father (a Navy officer) took a piece of scrap wood, centered it on the lathe and turned it into a beautiful new curved baluster that when painted and fitted into the railing, looked exactly like the original. From a piece of raw wood, his father had created something beautiful and enduring.

This made a lasting impression and was the inspiration for David's lifelong passion for carpentry. The seed was planted, and he began to construct things out of wood for his own use. His first projects included a door knocker shaped like a woodpecker, a sled made from old wooden skis and a bookcase with a built-in record player. Because he was self-taught, some of these initial attempts were crude and some failed entirely, like the Pogo boat he built with a friend, which sank upon christening. Others were learning experiences, like the clubhouse that was aborted at the framing stage—the lesson being to plan the joints on paper before investing in lumber! If this book had existed at that time, many problems could have been avoided.

Today, we spend our summers in a house (originally a barn) that we bought for $1,500 and have spent the last 25 years renovating with our own hands. We have built everything ourselves—the furniture, cabinets, tables, shelves, window seat, even the stone fireplace. Not only has our initial investment increased tenfold, but we've also had the pleasure of working together, designing and constructing things we're proud of and that are long-lasting.

With this in mind, we set out to write a book that would help anyone with a positive attitude acquire the basic skills of carpentry and successfully complete a variety of useful and interesting projects. Unlike most woodworking books, we have chosen projects that require a minimum of tools and are easy to build, usually in less than one day. They are well-designed, practical projects that will show off your craftsmanship and are durable enough to last a lifetime.

Getting Down
TO BASICS

WELCOME TO THE WORLD of woodworking. You are about to find out how wood can be manipulated and tooled into objects that can serve you the rest of your life. Like any other challenge, working with wood can be difficult. Wood has a mind or memory of its own, and it resists being coerced or shaped into a different form. The more you know about the characteristics and peculiarities of wood, the more successful you will be in your woodworking endeavors. By mastering a few basic building skills, you can transform rough lumber into a useful and aesthetically pleasing item and, at the same time, learn how the entire building process can be productive *and* rewarding.

Aptitudes & Attitudes

YOUR SKILL in carpentry is limited by two things: aptitude and attitude. You may think you don't have an aptitude for carpentry when, in fact, it is your *attitude* that is holding you back.

Attitudes are shaped by many things, beginning with early childhood. If you grew up in a household where hanging a picture frame or changing a flat tire created tense situations, filled with swearing and often resulting in frustration and failure, then you may have trouble facing these tasks yourself. Some kids are discouraged from building things with their hands and grow up with the misconception that excellence in manual skills is not a worthwhile goal. This is not true. There is nothing more relaxing and rewarding than involving yourself in a woodworking project—planning and designing it, building it and admiring your successful accomplishment upon completion.

Carpentry and woodworking today are not confined to only one type of person. "Shop" is often taught in schools to both boys and girls at an early age, and more and more women are finding that carpentry is not something limited only to men. Our niece, for example, a professional carpenter, is also a mother with three kids. With more electric tools on the market than ever before, physical strength is no longer a factor. Almost anyone who follows the basic instructions in this book should be able to perform most carpentry tasks successfully.

Just like a perfect golf swing or a good tennis stroke, sawing a straight, clean cut through a piece of lumber takes practice and concentration. Master carpenters, whose livelihoods depend upon making perfect cuts, develop an attitude based on total respect for the wood and the saw.

In Japan, for example, if an apprentice carpenter should happen to step over a saw, "his master would strike him soundly for showing such disrespect for his 'dogu' [tools]." (From *The Art of Japanese Joinery*, by Kiyosi Seike, Weatherhill/Tankosha Publishers, 1977.)

Regardless of one's reverence for wood, however, anyone can make mistakes—even the best of carpenters—and that's why it's important to approach a building project with a clear mind and focused attention.

The following are some of the most common mistakes people make in carpentry:
• Not taking enough time to plan and visualize how the pieces of wood will go together.
• Working in insufficient light.
• Not having all the necessary tools and lumber together before starting a project.
• Measuring incorrectly.
• Not checking to make sure both ends of a piece of lumber are square.
• Not checking as the work progresses to see if all the pieces are positioned correctly.
• Not clamping the wood securely to a stable work surface.
• Working at an uncomfortable height.
• Holding the hammer too close to the head.
• Not using a block under the hammer when removing nails.
• Using a too-large chisel.
• Sawing with uneven, jerky strokes.
• Using only one grade of sandpaper, instead of starting with coarse, graduating to medium and finishing with fine.

Design & Planning

THE FIRST FOUR building projects described in this book (the sawhorses, saw guide, nail box and toolbox) are not only simple projects to practice on, but they will also make any further building projects go more easily and quickly. Knowing where your tools and nails are, having sturdy sawhorses on which to create a work surface and using a saw guide to make accurate cuts not only increase your efficiency but also allow you to concentrate on the project at hand.

If you are adventuresome and decide to plan and build a project of your own design, keep the following tips in mind:

- Although wine-stained scribbles on a napkin may be the inspiration for your design, be sure to transfer them to a serious plan, using graph paper.
- Draw the plans to scale. For small projects, full-scale drawings are the most practical; however, for larger projects, 1 inch equals 1 foot is a good scale to use.
- For the serious designer, we suggest buying a three-sided architect's scale (each side has two different scales), a T-square, a 10-inch 45-degree triangle, and a protractor.
- When designing larger or more complicated projects, you may want to make a simple model or mock-up, using cardboard and white glue.

As you look through this book, you will notice projects that are accompanied by a construction drawing or plans, showing a side or end view and sometimes a top view or front view (see Fig. 1). Occasionally, reference is made to a section view (see Fig. 2), which appears as though a knife sliced through the object you are designing, exposing the inside. This view allows you to see how the piece

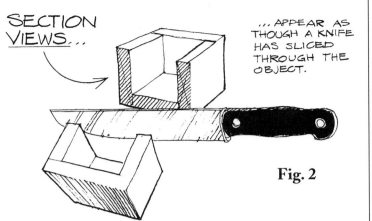

SECTION VIEWS...

...APPEAR AS THOUGH A KNIFE HAS SLICED THROUGH THE OBJECT.

Fig. 2

is constructed, and it is probably the most important view you can take. All residential architectural plans require this view because it is so revealing.

If you have occasion to study architectural or design plans, you may notice that they use abbreviations, symbols and conventions to conserve space on their drawings. We have also used symbols and abbreviations, which we have listed and defined in Fig. 3.

SOME DRAFTING SYMBOLS & ABBREVIATIONS USED IN THIS BOOK

Fig. 3

₵ OR —·—	=	CENTER LINE
— — — —	=	HIDDEN VIEW
	=	BROKEN VIEW
	=	CUT-AWAY SECTION
//	=	INCH
/	=	FOOT
ea.	=	EACH
&	=	AND
d. or DIA.	=	DIAMETER
R.	=	RADIUS
FIN.	=	FINISH (NAIL)
GALV.	=	GALVANIZED COATING
ELEC.	=	ELECTRIC
w/	=	WITH
VSR	=	VARIABLE-SPEED REVERSIBLE (DRILL)

Fig. 1

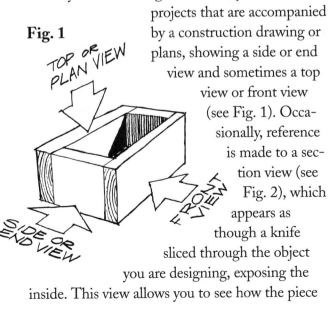

TOP OR PLAN VIEW

FRONT VIEW

SIDE OR END VIEW

Wood Wisdom

THE PIECE OF LUMBER you buy at a lumberyard will never forget that it was once part of a living tree. Because wood has a memory, lumber has a tendency to "cup" (see Fig. 4), especially when it is only ½ inch thick or is exceptionally wide, like a 1x12. One way to deal with this dilemma is to dampen the cupped side with a sponge and then clamp the board, cupped side down, to a flat surface or a flat board. Another way is to wipe the cupped side with a wet sponge, then turn it over and let it dry in the sun; this will straighten it out (see p. 13, Fig. 7).

A board can also twist (rack), bow or develop a crown—all defects that, hopefully, you will spot before buying your lumber and bringing it home! Also, look out for checks, split ends and excessive knots (see Fig. 4).

Wood has grain, or fibers, that run in only one direction. You should recognize this every time you pick up

Fig. 4

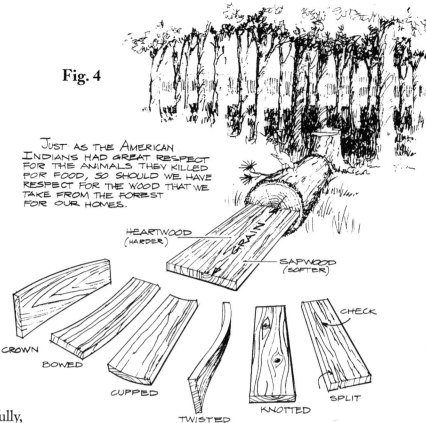

JUST AS THE AMERICAN INDIANS HAD GREAT RESPECT FOR THE ANIMALS THEY KILLED FOR FOOD, SO SHOULD WE HAVE RESPECT FOR THE WOOD THAT WE TAKE FROM THE FOREST FOR OUR HOMES.

Fig. 5

a piece of wood. It takes many blows with an ax to chop through a piece of wood across the grain but only a couple to split wood along, or with, the grain. Because wood splits so easily along the grain, you must be careful not to hammer large nails closely together in a row. The nails, with their wedge-shaped points, may split the board. Nails or screws put in too close to the edge of a thin board can also start a split (see Fig. 5).

Remember, too, that a board's orientation has a lot to do with how strong it is. For example, a board laid flat with a support under both ends may begin to sag in the middle; however, when it is placed "on edge," it is stronger, and stronger still when positioned "on end" (see Fig. 6). For additional information about wood, see Fig. 7.

WHEN A LOAD IS APPLIED   **Fig. 6**

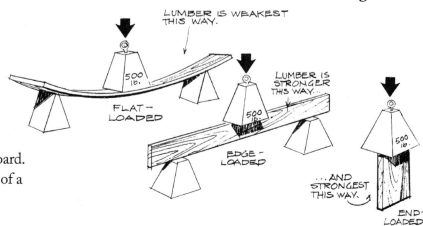

Fig. 7

FACTS TO KNOW ABOUT WOOD

- WOOD IS STRONGER BY WEIGHT THAN IRON.

- WOOD SHRINKS AND EXPANDS TEN TIMES AS MUCH ACROSS THE GRAIN AS WITH THE GRAIN.

ACROSS GRAIN

- SINCE THERE IS A NATURAL TENDENCY FOR WOOD TO CUP, SMART BUILDERS WILL LAY THEIR DECK BOARDS "CUP SIDE DOWN" SO THE RAIN WATER WILL RUN OFF.

- HEAVY WOOD BEAMS HOLD UP BETTER THAN WEBBED STEEL GIRDERS IN A VERY HOT FIRE.

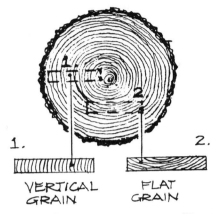

1.
VERTICAL GRAIN

2.
FLAT GRAIN

LUMBER CAN BE CUT OUT OF TREES IN TWO WAYS:

1. VERTICAL GRAIN – GOOD FOR DECKS, FLOORS OR IN SITUATIONS WHERE HEAVY LOADS ARE ANTICIPATED.

2. FLAT GRAIN – OFTEN HAS A MORE VARIED, INTERESTING GRAIN PATTERN (FIGURING).

- TERMITES CAN INFEST LUMBER THAT IS LEFT ON THE GROUND, EVEN IF THE LUMBER IS LEFT ON THE GROUND FOR JUST A FEW DAYS. NEITHER TERMITES NOR CARPENTER ANTS LIKE DRY WOOD, SO KEEP YOUR LUMBER DRY.

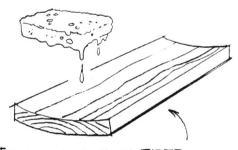

IF A BOARD IS CUPPED, WIPE IT WITH A WET SPONGE ON THE CONCAVE SIDE. TURN IT OVER AND LET IT DRY IN THE SUN AND IT WILL STRAIGHTEN OUT.

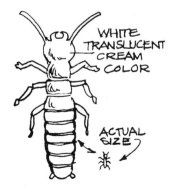

WHITE TRANSLUCENT CREAM COLOR

ACTUAL SIZE

WORKER TERMITE...SHUNS LIGHT

HOW TO PICK OUT LUMBER

Before going to the lumberyard, make a list of the supplies you will need for your project and write down the specifications for the lumber. Bring along your plans, a ¾-inch-wide by 16-foot-long measuring tape and a pencil to check off each item as you find it. The lumberyard experience can be daunting, so organize yourself before you arrive at the gate!

Don't be embarrassed to admit that you are a "beginner carpenter." Unless you drive a pickup truck and know everyone by their first name, it will be obvious, so there's no point in donning faded bib overalls and sporting a pencil above your ear to try to obtain a "contractor's discount." It won't work! Instead, take advantage of the lumber company's expert sales force. Arrive with a list of questions and don't be afraid to ask them. With your plans in hand, double-check the specifications for your project with the yard person, and ask to be directed to the available lumber.

Once you have been shown where the lumber is that fits your requirements, let the yard person know that you would like to pick out your own pieces from the pile. This can be a long, tedious process, especially with the sun blazing down on you or a freezing wind blowing in your face. But stick with it—it's worth it! And it certainly beats returning to the yard later with a piece of lumber that you didn't notice was badly warped or had numerous knots in it. In addition, many lumberyards charge a fee for returning lumber, so it pays to take your time.

To locate the board you want from the stacks, begin by pulling out each board and inspecting it. Hold each piece up on end to make sure that it is straight and free of knots and splits (see Fig. 8). If it doesn't pass inspection, slide it back onto a different row of lumber. To show respect for the lumberyard, always replace each board neatly, so

Fig. 8

that the butt ends line up and the boards are lying on the pile in a straight, orderly fashion.

Bring a handsaw with you to the lumberyard, in case there isn't a piece of lumber small enough for you. If you check with a yard person first, he or she will generally let you saw off a short length, as long as you leave at least 6 feet on the board. For instance, you can cut 4 feet off a 12-foot board, leaving the yard with an 8-foot length.

In some cases, you can drive your car right into the yard where the "stacks" are and load the lumber into or onto the car yourself. If you are buying only a few 8-foot-long boards and drive a station wagon, try wedging them between the seats, front to rear, saving you the time and effort of roping them to the roof. For larger loads, bring 30 to 40 feet of ¼-inch-diameter rope to tie the lumber to the roof of your car. If you don't have a rack on your roof, bring an old blanket to keep the lumber from scratching the top of your car (see Fig. 9). Using a "trucker's hitch" (see Fig. 10), tie the lumber onto the roof by opening the two front doors and running the rope through the car, just below the ceiling. Don't be afraid that you'll cut the rope when closing the doors: They will only pinch it, securing the rope tighter around the lumber.

When tying the materials to the roof of your car, be sure to lash down the front end of the

Fig. 9

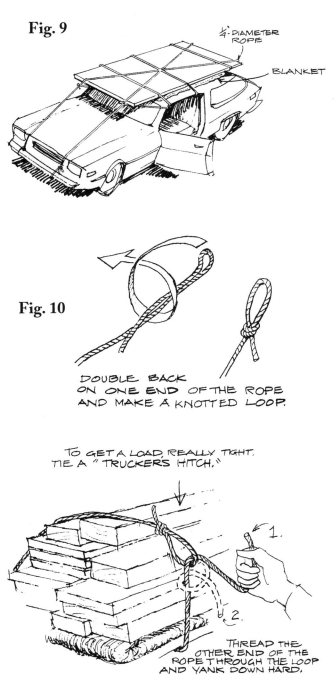

Fig. 10

DOUBLE BACK
ON ONE END OF THE ROPE
AND MAKE A KNOTTED LOOP.

TO GET A LOAD REALLY TIGHT,
TIE A "TRUCKERS HITCH."

THREAD THE
OTHER END OF THE
ROPE THROUGH THE LOOP
AND YANK DOWN HARD.

FINISH THE JOB BY
TYING IT OFF WITH A
HALF HITCH.

lumber tightly to prevent the wood from jack-knifing up if you suddenly put on the brakes. Always double-check the load to make sure that it is securely fastened down before leaving the lumberyard.

After picking out your lumber and loading it into or onto your car, the usual procedure is to go inside to the lumberyard's counter with a list of what you are taking. You should write down the exact amount of lumber, along with the thickness, width, length, grade and species. For example:

(3) three 1x6x8-foot #2 common pine boards

When driving home with a sheet of plywood on the roof, don't go over 50 mph, as the plywood could actually begin to act as an airfoil, lifting up off the roof of the car. Make sure the plywood is restrained by the rope so it won't slide forward if you brake suddenly. Start up slowly if you are on a hill, to prevent the plywood from sliding backward. If your load is longer than the car, attach a red flag to the back end of the lumber to avoid getting a traffic ticket (see Fig. 11).

Fig. 11

LUMBER SIZES

One of the first things you should be aware of is that the actual size of lumber does not match its description. In other words, a 2x4 does not actually measure out to be 2 inches by 4 inches. Instead, it is 1½ inches by 3½ inches. This is the result of the drying out and milling, or "dressing," process that the lumber goes through before it leaves the sawmill. Even plywood is often a fraction of an inch thinner than how it's described. This discrepancy in measurement may seem frustrating at first, but you'll soon adapt to it. It's essential to remain aware of this difference when planning your cuts in order to allow for the thickness of adjoining materials.

The following is a list of stock board lumber sizes:

Description	Actual Size
1x2	¾x1½ inches
1x3	¾x2½ inches
1x4	¾x3½ inches
1x6	¾x5½ inches
1x8	¾x7¼ inches
1x10	¾x9¼ inches
1x12*	¾x11¼ inches
½x4	⁷⁄₁₆x3½ inches
½x6*	⁷⁄₁₆x5½ inches
½x8*	⁷⁄₁₆x7¼ inches

* These extra-wide boards have a tendency to "cup."

TYPES OF LUMBER

When you walk into a lumberyard, you'll notice that lumber is either stored sheltered under a roof or shed or stacked in large, neat piles in the yard. The lumber stored outside, exposed to the rain and snow, is air-dried or "green" lumber and is stamped S-GRN. Air-dried lumber has more moisture content than kiln-dried wood and will shrink and warp as it ages. It is referred to as "2-by dimension" lumber (actually measuring 1½ inches), is thicker wood and is generally used for rough carpentry, beams and house framing. The lumber stored under a roof is typically kiln-dried, ¾-inch-thick "board" lumber stamped S-DRY or MC-15 and is used for finished carpentry. For most of the projects in this book, you will need kiln-dried wood, which is drier and more stable than air-dried lumber.

Most of our projects specify ¾-inch-thick boards, which are referred to as 1x2s, 1x3s, 1x4s, 1x6s, 1x8s, 1x10s and 1x12s. These boards come in two basic grades: clear, which is also referred to as "select" or "finish," meaning the board has a perfect, natural finish with no knots; and #2 lumber, which is also called "common" lumber, boards that contain some knots and imperfec-

tions in the wood. If you are painting your project, you can save money by using #2 common lumber, since a sealer and a good paint can be used to cover the knots. Both clear and common lumber include softwoods such as pine, spruce, fir and cedar.

Keep in mind that clear lumber costs almost three times as much as #2 common lumber. One trick is to buy extra-long lengths of #2 common lumber and use only the sections that are free of knots. This can save you a great deal of money, and the leftover pieces can be used where they don't show.

Most lumber is sold in 2-foot increments, starting with 6 feet and extending to 20 feet. Lumberyards generally spray the ends of the boards with colored paint to identify the board's length. For instance, in our lumberyard, yellow represents 8-foot lengths; silver, 10-foot; red, 12-foot; blue, 14-foot; and black, 16-foot. Often, there is a chart on a nearby wall that explains the color coding. Regardless of the length you need, you should always look for a nice, straight piece of lumber with as few defects as possible.

In addition to square-edged boards, there also are "tongue and groove" and "shiplap" boards, used for wall paneling or exterior siding. The projects in this book, however, require only square-edged boards.

SPECIALTY WOODS

Most of our projects can be made with clear or #2 common lumber; however, in some instances, you might want to use a specialty wood, like oak, redwood, mahogany, teak, birch, poplar, walnut, cherry, maple or cypress. These woods are more expensive, so if you need only a small piece, check with the lumberyard to see if you can cut off a 2- or 4-foot length from a 12-foot or longer board, as mentioned earlier. Specialty woods are stored under a roof and are generally sold by the lineal foot.

PLYWOOD

Plywood consists of several thin wood layers, or plies, glued together. Exterior plywood is made with waterproof glue. Generally fir or pine, exterior plywood is used in house construction and is commonly available at lumberyards in face grades of A, B and C. Grades of A and B are presanded. However, for cabinets, doors and paneling, where appearance is foremost, use a cabinet-grade plywood, which is not made with waterproof glue and is faced with an unblemished veneer of birch, oak or lauan. It can be made from other types of wood as well, but these are the ones most commonly available.

Plywood comes in both large (4x8-foot) and small (4x4-foot) sheets. The ease of handling the smaller size is worth the slight increase in price, and it might even fit into the back seat of your car. Choose a grade of plywood that has at least one good side, and use the good side for the exposed side of your project. Unless finished with an expensive hardwood veneer like birch or oak, the average fir plywood generally does not have an attractive appearance. Because plywood is made in multiple thin layers, or "plies," of wood, the swirly grain surface does not stain well. Plywood can be painted, but the edges will have an unfinished look to them unless they are covered with an iron-on plastic or wood edge banding

Fig. 12

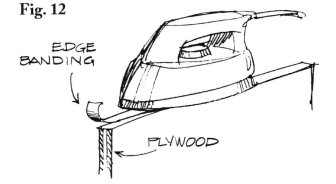

EDGE BANDING

PLYWOOD

(see Fig. 12). Another option is to fill the end grains with wood filler or vinyl spackle and lightly sand them. If you are going to paint the plywood, consider using MDO plywood, a weather-resistant exterior plywood with a smooth, waterproof finish that accepts paint well.

MOLDINGS

Moldings are a type of wood trim often used around window and door frames and along the base of walls. We have used them occasionally in this book to give a finished and professional look to a project, such as the Simple Shelf with Pegs (see p. 98). Although the shelf can be made without this extra touch, the piece is definitely more distinctive and interesting with nose and cove molding trimming the shelf.

Moldings are always cut from clear lumber and are stored under a roof, protected from the elements. Generally, lumberyards have a catalog that shows dimensions and drawings of the molding stock available. When selecting molding, consider the thickness, width and length of the piece. Most are available in pine and oak, and the more commonly available shapes include cove, lattice, base, crown, nose and half- and quarter-round moldings.

PRESSURE-TREATED (P.T.) WOOD

Pressure-treated wood is wood (most often southern pine) that has been treated under pressure (not just dipped) with a chemical referred to as CCA—the "A" standing for inorganic arsenic! Wear safety glasses and chemical-resistant vinyl-coated gloves when cutting or handling this material, and *never* use it indoors or burn it. It should not be placed near a vegetable garden or where it could leach into the drinking water.

The advantage of pressure-treated wood is that it is impervious to rot and insects and will last approximately 40 years. For this reason, it makes good picnic table legs or deck supports, since these posts are often sunk directly into the ground. Pressure-treated plywood is also available and is stored outside with the other P.T. lumber.

Safety Tips

No MATTER what you are building or whether you're using hand tools or power tools, safety should always be first and foremost in your mind. Here are some tips to help you cultivate safe working habits and maintain a safe building environment:

• Keep your mind on your work at all times and don't rush. When making repetitive cuts with an electric saw, approach each cut as though it were the first one, rethinking what you intend to do.
• Don't operate electric tools in wet conditions and don't ever use a two-prong extension cord. Use a grounded (three-prong) plug to provide electric power to the saw. Don't leave power tools plugged in after you have finished working.
• Always make sure the cord is out of the way before turning on any electric tool.
• Keep all cutting tools cleaned and well-sharpened. Sharper tools cut more easily and are actually safer to use.

• Wear safety goggles when operating power tools, especially when cutting plywood.
• When sawing lumber, either clamp it to a steady and sturdy work surface or set it on two solid supports, such as sawhorses. Never cut the lumber between the two supports, however, as this will cause the saw to bind and kick back suddenly (see p. 29, Fig. 35).
• Don't let young children operate power tools.
• Don't wear loose clothing, for it could become entangled with your tools or work. Also, wear shoes that will provide protection for your feet, in case a tool or a piece of lumber is accidentally dropped.
• Watch out for splinters when you are handling and working with plywood and other rough-sawn lumber.
• Make sure that the area in which you are working is well-lit and well-ventilated, especially when using wood finishes.
• Before standing on a ladder, first make sure it is steady and level at the base. Avoid standing on the top two rungs.
• Don't leave tools on top of a stepladder.
• Always clean up your building site at the end of the day and store your tools in a shed, workshop or other protected area. Secure the lids on cans of paint and finishes. Replace the tops on tubes of glue and construction adhesives and put them safely away.
• Keep a first-aid kit handy.

Tools & Carpentry
SKILLS

L ET'S ASSUME that you don't own a single tool and you want to buy a few basic ones. The following list contains the most essential tools, noted in order of importance. To help you find these tools, we have included a Sources section (see p. 147), listing several catalogs from which hardware, hand and power tools can be ordered.

Basic Tools

- ¾-inch-wide, 16-foot-long steel tape measure (see Fig. 1)
- Combination square (see Fig. 2)
- 13-ounce claw hammer (see Fig. 3)
- Crosscut saw (see Fig. 4)
- Electric jigsaw (see Fig. 5)
- Two standard (slotted) screwdrivers (4 inch and 6 inch) and two Phillips screwdrivers (4 inch and 6 inch; see Fig. 6)
- ⅜-inch electric variable-speed, reversible (VSR) drill with standard and Phillips-head bits (see Fig. 7)
- One each: ¼-inch, ½-inch and ¾-inch wood chisels (see Fig. 8)
- One set of twist drill bits: ¹⁄₁₆ inch, ⅛ inch, ³⁄₁₆ inch, ¼ inch and ⁵⁄₁₆ inch (see Fig. 9)
- One set of flat spade drill bits: ⅜ inch, ½ inch, ⅝ inch, ¾ inch, ⅞ inch, 1 inch, 1¼ inches, 1⅜ inches and 1½ inches (see Fig. 10)
- Two 10-inch hand-screw wood clamps (see Fig. 11)
- Four-in-hand (combination file and rasp; see Fig. 12)
- Nail set (see Fig. 13)

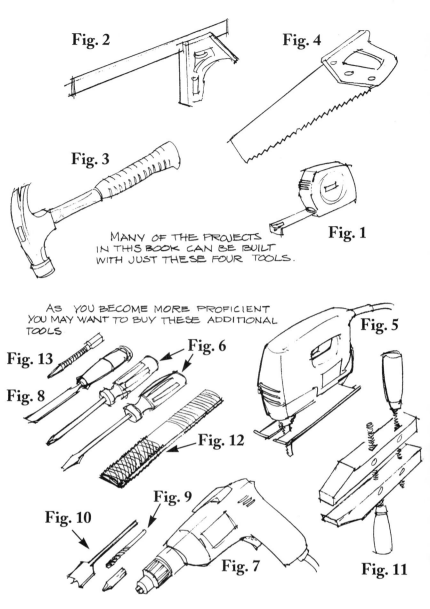

MANY OF THE PROJECTS IN THIS BOOK CAN BE BUILT WITH JUST THESE FOUR TOOLS.

AS YOU BECOME MORE PROFICIENT YOU MAY WANT TO BUY THESE ADDITIONAL TOOLS

Measuring

TAPE MEASURE

(see Figs. 14A and 14B)

When buying a steel tape measure, an important consideration is its width—it should be at least ¾ inch wide. Some carpenters test tape measures by how long they can be extended without collapsing. My ½-inch by 12-foot tape will extend only about 3 feet before collapsing, while my ¾-inch one will extend 7 feet. This becomes very important when you are working alone. Even measuring for your Christmas tree, from the floor to ceiling, can be an impossible task without the right tape measure!

Most tapes are calibrated with marks at every 16 inches on-center. This is done to help you locate studs in a wall, which are 16 inches apart in most houses, although some may be 24 inches.

Notice that there is an "end hook" on the tape measure. This hook is loosely riveted in order to adjust for an "inside" or an "outside" measurement. Be careful not to get the rivets caught on the edge of the piece that you are measuring. When taking an inside measurement (see Detail,

Fig. 14A

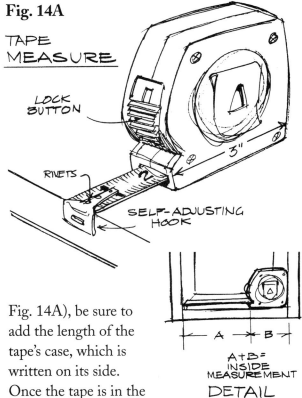

TAPE MEASURE

LOCK BUTTON

RIVETS

SELF-ADJUSTING HOOK

A + B = INSIDE MEASUREMENT

DETAIL

Fig. 14A), be sure to add the length of the tape's case, which is written on its side. Once the tape is in the correct position for measuring, slide the lock button in place.

The most important lesson to learn when taking measurements is to measure accurately and to *always* measure twice. Even some of the best carpenters occasionally make mistakes while measuring, and the results can be disastrous. Hurrying to get started on a project can add hours to the construction process, as you'll later need to correct the mistakes that result from inaccurate measurements. An old adage to remember is "Measure twice and cut once." This is as true today as it ever was, whether using old-fashioned hand tools or state-of-the-art electric tools.

A useful trick David learned is to always mark your measurement so that it is clear which side of the mark is the "waste" side. Using a sharp pencil, make a heavy, dark "cut" line, and to the waste side of this line, make a lighter line 1/16 to 1/8 inch (the width of a saw blade) next to the first line.

This helps you to line up the saw on the correct side of the cutting mark.

Another thing to watch out for is reading the numbers on the tape upside down. The number 16 looks like a 91 when viewed upside down, and 21 can be mistaken for 12. Adding a series of incorrectly read numbers can easily result in the waste of an expensive piece of lumber, so always take the time to double-check your work.

Some other helpful measuring tips:
• Line the tape up parallel with the edge of whatever you are measuring. To make a more accurate mark, twist the tape measure so that the tape's edge lies flat on the board (see Fig. 14B).
• Jot down all measurements on a piece of paper, even if you think they are easy to remember.
• Never substitute a cloth tape measure for a steel one, because cloth stretches and will give you a false reading.

Fig. 14B

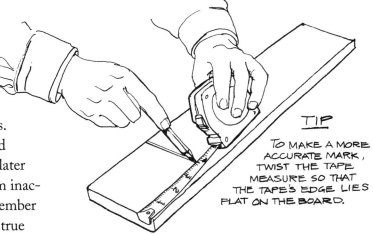

TIP
TO MAKE A MORE ACCURATE MARK, TWIST THE TAPE MEASURE SO THAT THE TAPE'S EDGE LIES FLAT ON THE BOARD.

COMBINATION SQUARE
(see Fig. 15)

If you watch professional carpenters at work, you'll notice that every so often they will stop and recheck their project's measurements with a combination square. This is a good habit to get into, since quite often a project will get "out of square" during the building process.

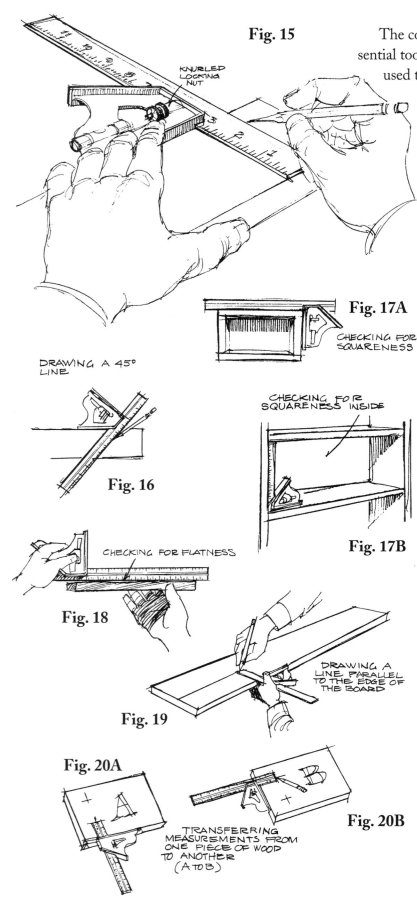

Fig. 15

KNURLED LOCKING NUT

Fig. 17A

CHECKING FOR SQUARENESS

DRAWING A 45° LINE

CHECKING FOR SQUARENESS INSIDE

Fig. 16

Fig. 17B

CHECKING FOR FLATNESS

Fig. 18

DRAWING A LINE PARALLEL TO THE EDGE OF THE BOARD

Fig. 19

Fig. 20A

Fig. 20B

TRANSFERRING MEASUREMENTS FROM ONE PIECE OF WOOD TO ANOTHER (A TO B)

The combination square is one of the most essential tools to have in your toolbox. It can be used to measure small objects, to mark cuts at 45-degree (mitered) angles (see Fig. 16) and 90-degree (right) angles, to measure the depth of a mortised hole and to check that an object is square or flat (see Figs. 17A and 17B and Fig. 18).

It is also useful for drawing parallel lines (see Fig. 19). You can even use a combination square to take measurements and transfer them to another piece of wood without reading the numbers. Do this by loosening the knurled nut and sliding the rule forward until the end of the rule lines up with the point you are measuring on the first piece of wood (see Fig. 20A). Tighten the nut and move the combination square to the new piece of wood, marking at the end of the rule (see Fig. 20B).

Other useful squares that you may want to add to your toolbox as you gain more experience include:

FRAMING SQUARE

(see Fig. 21)

A framing, or carpenter's, square is made from one piece of steel or aluminum with measurements marked along the inside and the outside of its two legs. The 2x24-inch leg is referred to as the "blade" and the 1½x16-inch leg is called the "tongue." The two legs meet at a 90-degree angle at the "heel." When purchasing a framing square, be sure it is rust-resistant and that the numbers are incised into the surface of the metal.

The framing square, which is longer than the combination square, is more practical when building large projects. It is used to mark straight lines across boards and to check for squareness on projects such as cabinets, doors, workbenches and sheds. Be careful not to step on, drop or bang this square, since accuracy depends on its exact shape. When laying out projects using 2x4s (1½x3½ inches), it is helpful to remember that the "tongue" of the square is 1½ inches wide.

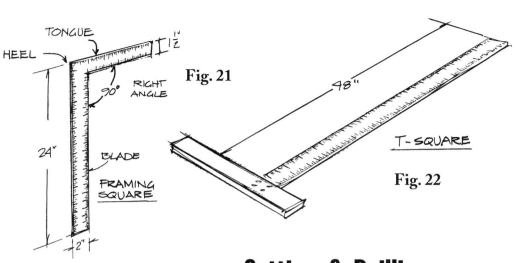

Fig. 21

Fig. 22

T-Square

(see Fig. 22)

A T-square is generally thought to be a draftsman's tool, but today it comes in 48-inch lengths and can be used for measuring, marking and cutting drywall and other sheet materials such as plywood. It is made of aluminum.

Speed Square

(see Fig. 23)

A speed square is a durable, multipurpose tool. It can be used for marking right-angle cuts, and its thick edge makes it especially handy as a saw guide when cutting lumber with a portable circular saw. It is quite popular among house carpenters because it won't break or bend if stepped on.

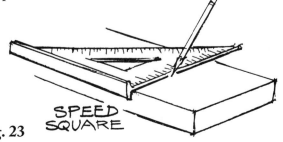

Fig. 23

Cutting & Drilling

HANDSAWS

(see Fig. 24)

Saws come in all shapes and sizes and are used for different purposes; the most common is the traditional crosscut saw. A similar saw was first used by the Egyptians more than 5,000 years ago. Whether you have inherited a handsaw, found one at a yard sale or bought a new one, you should take it to your local hardware store or lumberyard and have it sharpened. Nothing dulls the enthusiasm of an aspiring carpenter as much as struggling with a dull saw.

If you don't own a handsaw and are hesitant about investing a lot of money in one, we recommend buying a crosscut saw made by Stanley called the Short Cut. Only 18 inches long (shorter than most crosscut saws), it fits neatly into a toolbox and has a unique "set" to the teeth that allows you to cut on both the forward and the back stroke. With eight teeth to the inch, it makes fairly coarse cuts, but this is offset by the fact that it cuts so quickly and effortlessly. Another clever feature is that the handle doubles as a marking square for drawing right angles. In addition to its uses as a crosscut saw, we also use our Stanley Short Cut for pruning shrubs and small tree branches, and it can serve as a ripsaw, too, if necessary.

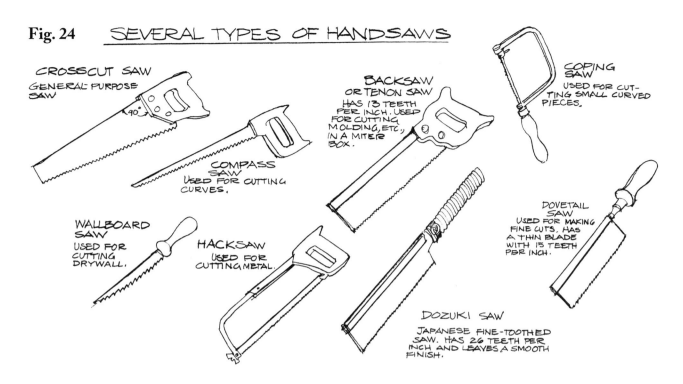

Fig. 24 SEVERAL TYPES OF HANDSAWS

CROSSCUT SAW
GENERAL PURPOSE SAW
90°

COMPASS SAW
USED FOR CUTTING CURVES.

BACKSAW OR TENON SAW
HAS 13 TEETH PER INCH. USED FOR CUTTING MOLDING, ETC., IN A MITER BOX.

COPING SAW
USED FOR CUTTING SMALL CURVED PIECES.

WALLBOARD SAW
USED FOR CUTTING DRYWALL.

HACKSAW
USED FOR CUTTING METAL.

DOVETAIL SAW
USED FOR MAKING FINE CUTS. HAS A THIN BLADE WITH 15 TEETH PER INCH.

DOZUKI SAW
JAPANESE FINE-TOOTHED SAW. HAS 26 TEETH PER INCH AND LEAVES A SMOOTH FINISH.

The ripsaw is another type of handsaw—used only for "rip" cuts, which are made with the grain of the wood. The teeth of the ripsaw are larger than those of the crosscut's and are shaped so that the front of each tooth is at a 90-degree angle (see Fig. 25). The traditional crosscut saw, on the other hand, has small teeth that are slightly slanted back. The ripsaw cuts wood along the grain, while the crosscut saw—as the name implies—cuts wood across the grain (and through plywood). In a pinch, you can use a crosscut saw to cut with the grain, but you can't use a ripsaw to cut across the grain. Therefore, if you are investing in only one saw, a crosscut saw is the better choice.

Fig. 25

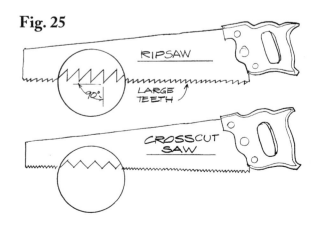

RIPSAW
90°
LARGE TEETH

CROSSCUT SAW

Cutting lumber with a handsaw:

Before you start cutting, you must first measure and mark a cut line on the board. Place a combination square flush against the edge of the board, and holding the square firmly with one hand, draw a line across the board, using the edge of the square as your guide (see p. 22, Fig. 15). To help you remember which side of the line is the waste side, use David's technique of drawing two lines as described on p. 21.

If possible, clamp the board you are cutting to a strong base support; otherwise, brace the board with your knee and your free hand (see Fig. 26A). A chair, stool, low sawhorse or other suitable work surface positioned so that it is between knee and knuckle height makes a comfortable base for handsawing (see Fig. 26B). A support that is too high makes sawing difficult, since it places your wrist in an awkward, weak position (see Fig. 26C). If the support is too low, the tip of the saw may hit the ground (see Fig. 26D).

Position yourself so that the arm that you are sawing with is in line with the saw and the cut

POSITION IS VERY IMPORTANT WHEN SAWING BY HAND.

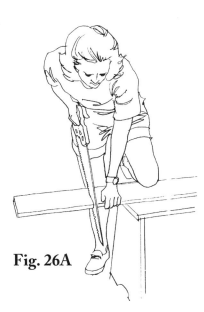

Fig. 26A

Fig. 26B

A GOOD SUPPORT HEIGHT FOR WORKING IS BETWEEN KNEE AND KNUCKLE HEIGHT WHEN STANDING UP STRAIGHT.

DON'T TRY TO SAW A BOARD USING A TABLE THAT IS TOO HIGH...

Fig. 26C

... OR A TABLE THAT IS TOO LOW.

Fig. 26D

Fig. 27

line. If you are right-handed, your right eye should be directly over the beginning of the cut line. Grasp the saw handle firmly with a straight wrist, resting the saw blade on the cut line. Hold the saw at a 45-degree angle and start the cut by pulling the saw back toward you, using a very short movement. (Because the saw teeth are facing forward, it is easier to make the beginning cut in the wood by first pulling back on the saw rather than pushing forward.) Make a small cut in the board, check to see if it is on the cut line, then continue sawing.

As the cut progresses, the saw strokes should become longer and more force should be given to the forward stroke, away from your body. This is the stroke that actually does the cutting. As you cut through the board, stop occasionally and check to see if you are on the cut line. If not, move the saw back a few inches and bring the cut back onto the line. (Hopefully, any mistakes will be on the "waste" side of the line.)

If possible, have a helper lightly support the waste end of the wood, so that it doesn't drop off, splitting the end of the wood (see Fig. 27). Make sure that your assistant doesn't lift up on the wood, as this can cause the saw blade to bind.

If you are rip-cutting (cutting with the grain of the wood), you can saw more efficiently and quickly by holding the handsaw at a steeper or more upright angle.

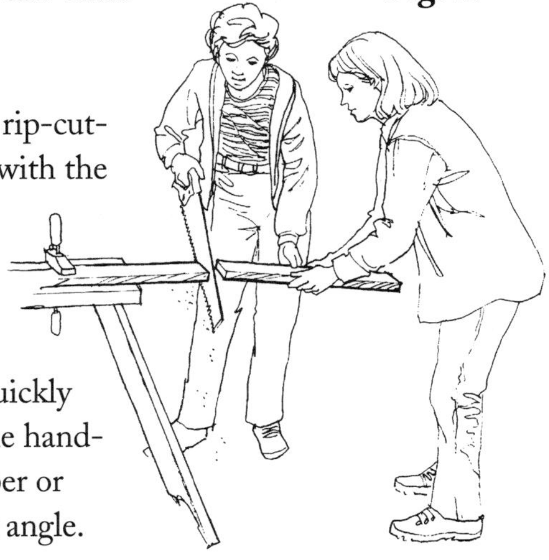

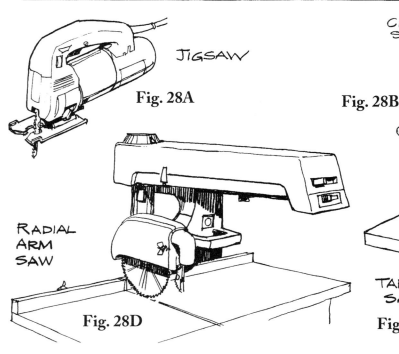

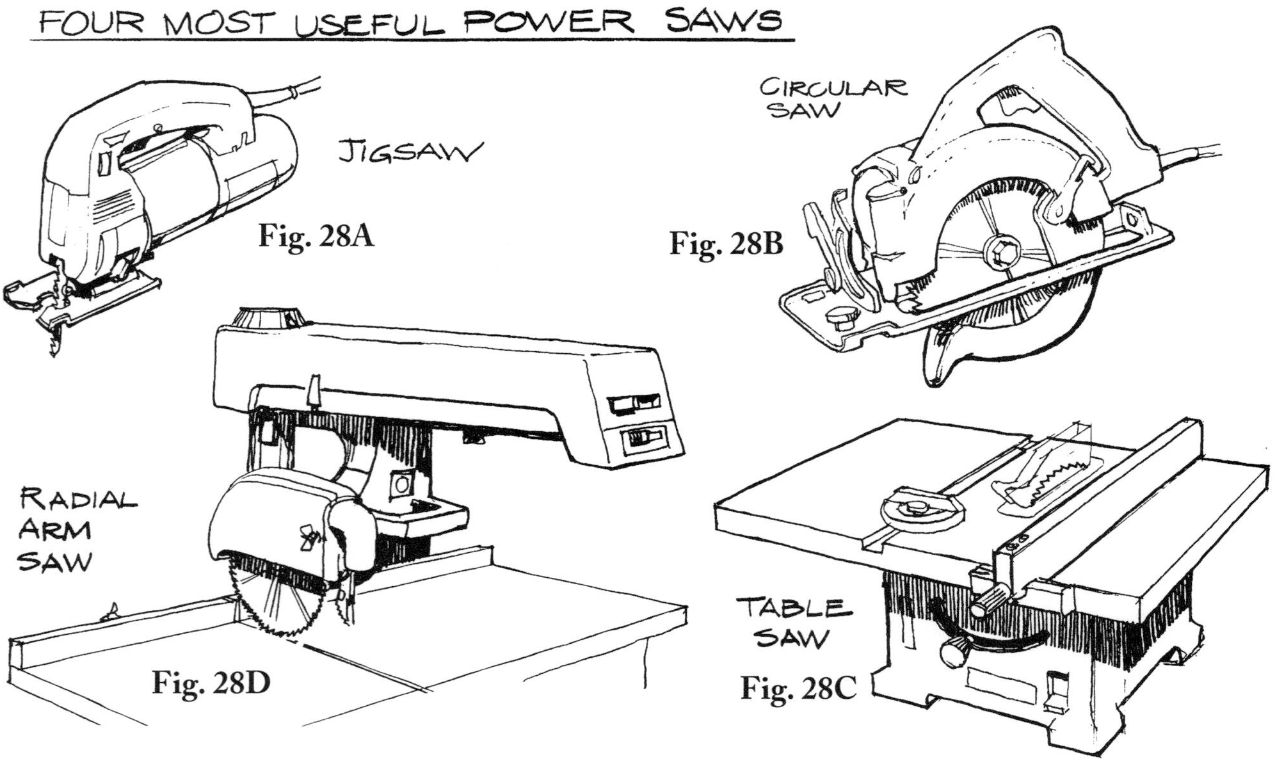

FOUR MOST USEFUL POWER SAWS

JIGSAW
Fig. 28A

CIRCULAR SAW
Fig. 28B

RADIAL ARM SAW
Fig. 28D

TABLE SAW
Fig. 28C

POWER SAWS

(see Figs. 28A through 28D)

Since power tools operate at very high speeds, they can be dangerous if not handled correctly. Before even turning on a power saw, check that the electric cord is out of the way of the saw blade and that the work area is clear of any possible obstructions. Also, make a habit of stopping for a moment from time to time and looking around you to see that everything is safe and in its proper position. Always wear safety goggles or glasses when using these power tools.

Electric Jigsaw

(see Fig. 28A)

If you plan on building more than five projects in this book, we suggest buying an electric jigsaw. Of all the power saws, it is the least expensive, the quietest, the least dangerous and, therefore, the *easiest* to use. Unlike the other power saws, it also has the advantage of being able to cut curves. Choose an electric jigsaw with variable speeds, which provides you with more options.

You will probably want to buy additional blades from the manufacturer of the saw. We advise changing them as soon as the saw blade becomes dull and starts to cut slowly. If you are interested in making a lifetime investment, we recommend the Bosch 1587DVS, a heavy-duty jigsaw that sells for around $150. It makes very precise, smooth cuts and automatically blows the sawdust away from the work surface. This is our favorite tool in the shop and the one we use most often for cutting wood.

Sawing with an electric jigsaw:

One of the advantages of an electric jigsaw is its ability to cut both curved and straight lines in wood. Before beginning a cut, position and clamp the wood to a table or sturdy work surface, placing the less desirable side of the wood face-up. The section to be cut off should extend past the edge of the table by at least an inch (see Fig. 29).

If you are making a straight cut, make a mark with a pencil at the measurement to be cut and place a combination square flush against the edge of the board at this mark. Holding the square firmly with one hand, draw a line across the board, using the edge of the square as your guide (see p. 22, Fig. 15). Remove the square and place the front of the foot plate of the jigsaw on the material to be cut (see Fig. 29).

Fig. 29

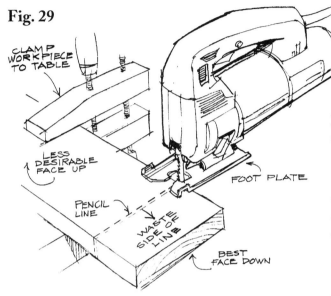

CLAMP WORKPIECE TO TABLE

LESS DESIRABLE FACE UP

FOOT PLATE

PENCIL LINE

WASTE SIDE OF LINE

BEST FACE DOWN

Never assume that you can make a straight cut with a jigsaw without using a speed square as a guide for the saw. After you have lined the saw up with the cut mark, position the speed square so that the lip of the square overlaps the top edge of the board and the remaining leg is flush

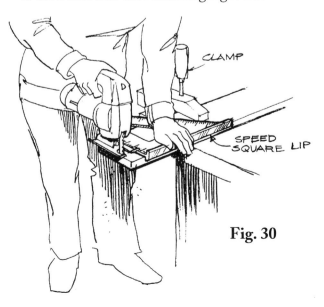

CLAMP

SPEED SQUARE LIP

Fig. 30

against the foot plate of the jigsaw (see Fig. 30). Make sure the saw blade is lined up with, but not touching, the cut line before turning on the saw.

Turn the saw on by gradually squeezing the trigger. Move the saw forward slowly until the blade enters the wood. Check to make sure that you are cutting on the "waste" side of the wood. Keep a firm grip and press down, resisting the tendency of the saw to "hop" up. Keep the saw firmly pressed down against the wood during cutting. In order to best see what you are cutting, keep your shoulders and your eyes in front of the saw, and always wear safety goggles or glasses.

Be aware that the blade will be exposed underneath the wood, so make sure that this area is clear. Never reach underneath your work while the saw is on.

When you have finished cutting, always unplug your saw. Test the accuracy of a straight cut by standing the piece on a level surface. If you see any high spots, remove them, using the jigsaw, a file or coarse (40-grit) sandpaper wrapped around a 1x4 sanding block (see p. 53-54, Figs. 78 and 79).

Occasionally, you may find that you need to cut a piece of wood that is too small to clamp to a work surface. You can solve this problem by clamping the entire board and cutting the smaller piece or pieces off first (see p. 99, Simple Shelf with Pegs, Fig. 3).

If you are cutting out a shape or design inside a board or panel, first draw the shape on the material to be cut. Drill a hole inside the area that will be cut out, using a ½-inch spade bit. Insert the saw blade in the hole before turning on the jigsaw. If you need to cut sharp corners for a square shape, make them round to begin with (see Fig. 31), then go back and square them off,

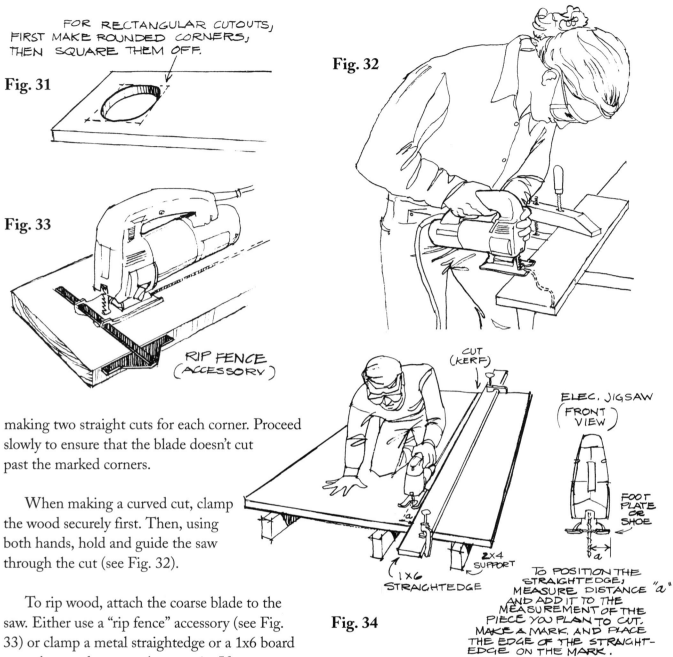

FOR RECTANGULAR CUTOUTS,
FIRST MAKE ROUNDED CORNERS,
THEN SQUARE THEM OFF.

Fig. 31

Fig. 33

RIP FENCE
(ACCESSORY)

Fig. 32

CUT
(KERF)

ELEC. JIGSAW
(FRONT VIEW)

FOOT PLATE OR SHOE

1X6 STRAIGHTEDGE

2X4 SUPPORT

TO POSITION THE
STRAIGHTEDGE,
MEASURE DISTANCE "a"
AND ADD IT TO THE
MEASUREMENT OF THE
PIECE YOU PLAN TO CUT.
MAKE A MARK, AND PLACE
THE EDGE OF THE STRAIGHT-
EDGE ON THE MARK.

Fig. 34

making two straight cuts for each corner. Proceed slowly to ensure that the blade doesn't cut past the marked corners.

When making a curved cut, clamp the wood securely first. Then, using both hands, hold and guide the saw through the cut (see Fig. 32).

To rip wood, attach the coarse blade to the saw. Either use a "rip fence" accessory (see Fig. 33) or clamp a metal straightedge or a 1x6 board onto the wood you are about to rip. If you are using the 1x6 board as your straightedge, make sure that it is perfectly straight. Allow for the extra dimension of the foot plate when positioning and clamping the straightedge to the wood to be cut (see Fig. 34). While rip-cutting, *always* keep the saw pressed down and against the straightedge to achieve a continuous straight cut. Make sure the saw blade remains vertical while sawing through the wood, and remember, ripping wood takes more time than crosscutting.

Portable Circular Saw (or Skilsaw)
(see p. 26, Fig. 28B)

Years ago, David built a cabin in the woods using only hand tools, and although he got a great deal of satisfaction and pride from not polluting the woods with the screeching sound of a portable circular saw ("sidewinder"), it took several years to finish. Today, with the aid of electricity, the same cabin could easily be built in a month.

Our favorite portable circular saw is relatively lightweight and has a 6-inch blade. If you are right-handed, it is especially helpful to be able to see the blade as it cuts the wood, since the blade is mounted on the left side of the saw. The portable circular saw is the tool of choice for such projects as decks and sheds, and it is absolutely essential for house building. The advantage of using a portable circular saw over handsawing is that ripping through long boards or cutting sheets of plywood takes seconds, rather than 10 to 15 minutes.

Cutting with a portable circular saw:

Making crosscuts with a portable circular saw is much faster than with any of the previously mentioned tools, but certain safety precautions should be observed. When crosscutting lumber, make sure that the piece you are cutting falls away from, not toward, the saw blade; otherwise, this can pinch the blade and cause it to kick back dangerously toward you. For instance, never place a piece of lumber over two sawhorses and then cut between them (see Fig. 35). Instead, position the lumber over the sawhorses so that the portion to be cut off is unsupported and will fall away from the outside edge of the saw blade (see Fig. 36). If you can, have a helper catch the cut-off piece of lumber before it falls to the ground.

To make your saw cuts perfectly square or straight, you might want to invest in a speed square (see Fig. 37), which is used for straight cuts, or a combination protractor/saw guide, more commonly referred to as an adjustable square (see Fig. 38), which can be used for straight cuts or adjusted for angled cuts.

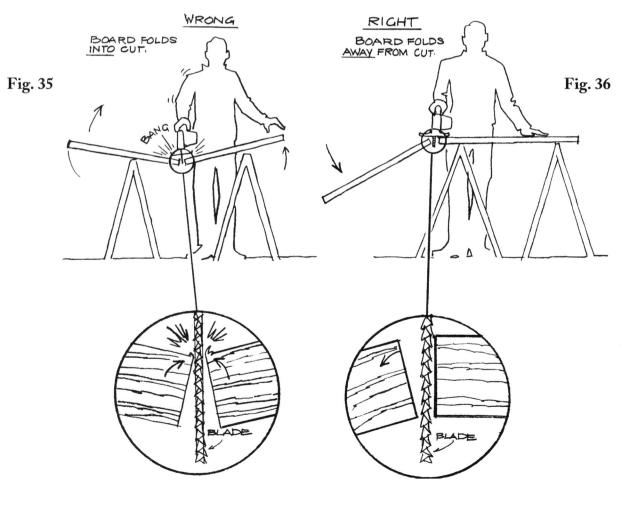

Fig. 35

WRONG

BOARD FOLDS INTO CUT.

BANG

BLADE

Fig. 36

RIGHT

BOARD FOLDS AWAY FROM CUT.

BLADE

Both of these measuring tools have one leg that rests on the edge of the board and another at a 90-degree angle to the first leg, which the foot (base) plate rides along. To use as a cutting guide, hold the square tightly against the upper edge of the wood you are cutting, while continuously keeping the shoe (base) of your power saw pressed against the guide as you make the cut.

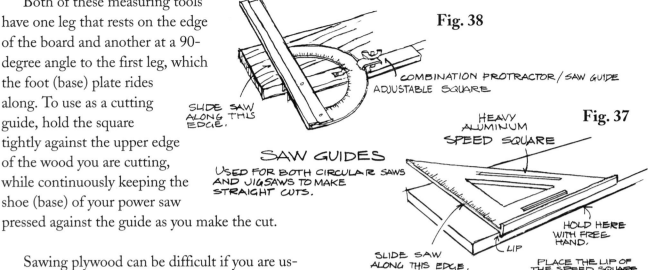

Fig. 38

COMBINATION PROTRACTOR / SAW GUIDE
ADJUSTABLE SQUARE

SLIDE SAW ALONG THIS EDGE.

SAW GUIDES
USED FOR BOTH CIRCULAR SAWS AND JIGSAWS TO MAKE STRAIGHT CUTS.

Fig. 37

HEAVY ALUMINUM SPEED SQUARE

HOLD HERE WITH FREE HAND.

SLIDE SAW ALONG THIS EDGE.

LIP

PLACE THE LIP OF THE SPEED SQUARE OVER THE EDGE OF THE BOARD.

Sawing plywood can be difficult if you are using a standard 4x8-foot sheet. Most lumberyards, however, will cut up a full-size sheet to your specifications, but you need to give them your cutting plan and pay a nominal milling fee.

If you want to cut the plywood yourself, buy a straight piece of 1x6 to act as a guide (see p. 28, Fig. 34). If you are sawing the plywood with a handsaw, place the panel on supports that are high enough to keep the nose of the saw from hitting the ground. Mark the cut line using a straight board or snap a line with a chalk line (see Fig. 39), which can be bought from a hardware store. Make sure the plywood sheet is supported so that it will not fall when you are finished with the cut. **TIP:** Before you begin cutting, give your saw blade a shot of silicone spray to make the saw glide more easily.

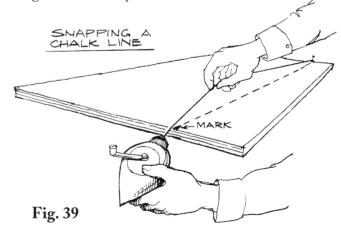

SNAPPING A CHALK LINE

MARK

Fig. 39

OTHER POWER SAWS

These are definitely serious machinery for doing professional work. The table saw (see p. 26, Fig. 28C) is the favorite of most shop carpenters because it is so accurate and has such versatility. It can even be fitted with a sanding disk, so you can give your projects a finished, professional look.

One thing a table saw can't do well is crosscuts. For this job, a radial arm saw (see p. 26, Fig. 28D) comes in handy. We have both, and keep a ripsaw blade on the table saw and a crosscut blade on the radial arm saw. Both saws are high-speed, expensive tools and can't be beat for accuracy. We resisted the temptation to use them while building the projects in this book, because we wanted to stick with simpler hand tools that wouldn't be costly.

Entire books have been written about the many types of electric table saws and radial arm saws. These advanced and versatile tools should be used only after thoroughly familiarizing yourself with the instructions. Other power saws include the reciprocating saw, the band saw, the "chop" miter saw and the chain saw.

Tear-Out

"Tear-out" is the term given to the tiny splinters left on the edge of plywood after the saw blade has cut through it. Whether you are using a handsaw or a table saw, you won't see the tear-out until you turn the sheet of plywood over, since the splintered edges only appear on the exit side. It is especially noticeable if you are cutting across the grain of plywood, and it can give you a handful of splinters if you're not careful.

When cutting with a portable circular saw or an electric jigsaw, cut the plywood with the good side down. If you are using a table saw or a radial arm saw, the opposite is true: The good side of the wood should face up. The important thing to remember is that the teeth of the saw blade should enter the good side of the plywood and exit the bad side.

Tear-out can be minimized by using a finer-toothed saw (13 teeth to the inch) or by holding the saw at a shallow angle to your work. The best way to prevent tear-out, however, is to use a utility knife to score two parallel cuts on either side of the saw exit line, just deep enough to sever the wood fibers of the first "ply" of the plywood. If you are using a jigsaw or a portable circular saw, make the score cuts on the top side of the plywood, since the good side of the wood faces down and the saw blade teeth will be exiting through the top surface. If you are using a handsaw, table saw or radial arm saw, score on the bottom side of the wood, since the good side of the wood faces up.

ELECTRIC DRILLS

(see Fig. 40)

It is impossible to know when the first drill was invented; however, we do know that primitive man burned holes through wood to make a hole. On a visit to the Egyptian Room at the Metropolitan Museum of Art in New York, we spotted something that looked very familiar. On the floor was a rough-hewn sledge built 4,000 years ago, used for hauling huge sarcophagi, or stone coffins. The sled was made of heavy timbers carefully joined with wooden pegs. What caught our eyes was the familiar cross mark that the ancient carpenter had made on the wood to indicate where the hole should be "drilled." David had drawn a similar cross mark that morning, for the same reason, on some architectural drawings. A crude form of metal drills existed even back then. The ancient Egyptians must have spent several hours making one hole, while today, we can do the same thing in seconds, using a speed drill (see Fig. 40).

Fig. 40

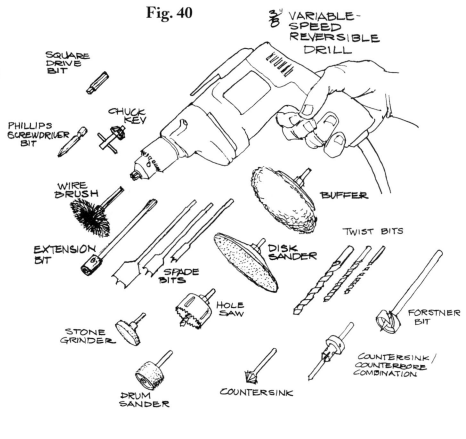

Today's tools have become so sophisticated that the brace-and-bit or hand-operated drill that you may have inherited could eventually become a collector's item! These "antique" boring tools have been replaced by what is perhaps the most useful tool that one can own: a variable-speed, reversible (VSR) electric drill. This versatile tool can be used for a variety of tasks. When fitted with a screwdriver bit, for example, it can eliminate the frustration of trying to screw into hardwoods like oak or maple. David still remembers trying to get four screws into a pair of maple skis by hand, and finding it an almost impossible task. It used to take hours to build things using hand tools and slotted screws. Today, with Phillips-head screws and a ⅜-inch VSR drill, screws can be drilled into wood in minutes—and removed just as easily should you need to reposition them.

In addition to drilling holes and screwing screws, electric drills can be fitted with several other attachments (see Fig. 40), such as a sanding disk for rotary sanding, a rotary drum for sanding inside tight curves, a wire brush for removing rust, a buffer for polishing the car or a countersink for sinking screws. There are even attachments for stirring paint and trimming shrubs.

Cordless battery-operated drills are another option, but be sure to buy one that is strong enough, at least 9 volts. To test for this, put on a leather glove and hold the "chuck" while you turn on the drill. A strong drill should be difficult, if not impossible, to keep from turning. In the earliest stages of development, cordless drills were a disappointment because their batteries could not hold a charge for long. But improvements have made it possible to use these drills for up to an hour. It is a nuisance, of course, when the drill runs completely out of power, but this will rarely happen if you remember to remove the battery from the drill and place the battery in the charger after each use.

Recent models come with a keyless chuck, which makes it easier to change bits.

TIP: When drilling large holes, especially through plywood, the surface of the wood where the drill exits is likely to split. To avoid this, drill only far enough through the first side so that you can see a hole made by the point of the drill on the back. Turn the board over, and using the small hole as a guide for the drill, finish drilling the hole completely through (see Fig. 41).

Fig. 41

HOLD BOARD WITH FOOT.

DRILL HALFWAY THROUGH UNTIL POINT OF SPADE BIT PROTRUDES SLIGHTLY FROM UNDERSIDE OF BOARD.

TURN BOARD OVER AND DRILL THROUGH FROM THE OTHER SIDE.

CHISELS

(see Figs. 42 through 46)

A wood chisel is often used in woodworking for making joints or shaping wood. A set of three plastic-handled chisels, ¼ inch, ½ inch and ¾ inch, should take care of all your needs and last you a lifetime. (Stanley makes excellent ones.)

Contrary to what you might expect, we have found that using a chisel that is too big is slower than using a small one. The wider the chisel blade, the more difficult it is for it to penetrate the wood. If you plan on buying only one chisel, we recommend choosing one with a ¼-inch blade.

MEASURING, HAMMER AND NAILS, DRILLS, CHISELS (PAGES 20, 43 AND 44, 31 AND 32)

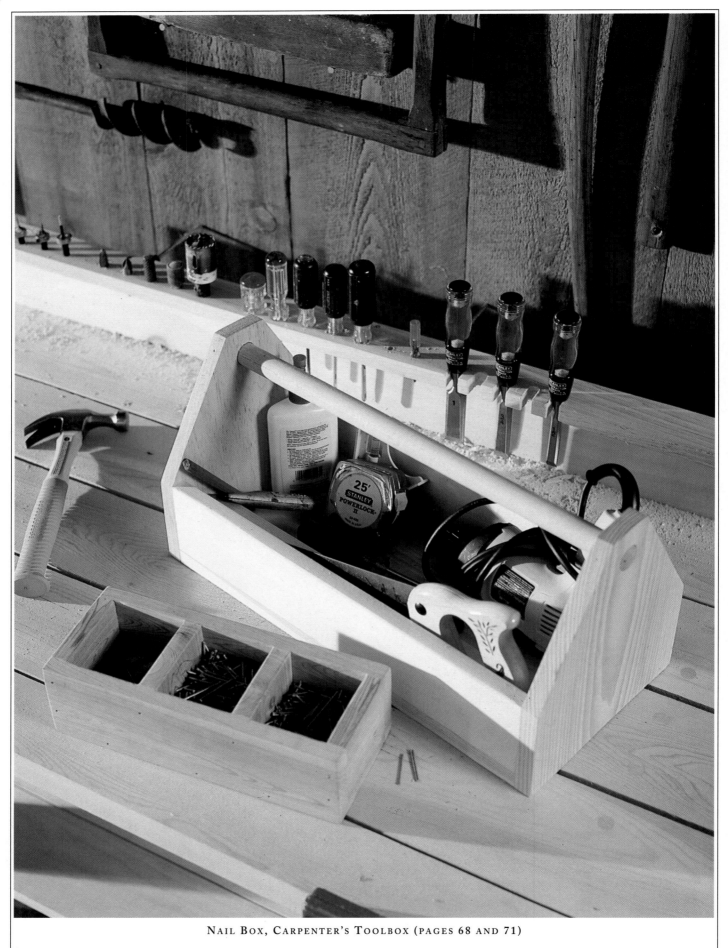

NAIL BOX, CARPENTER'S TOOLBOX (PAGES 68 AND 71)

ADJUSTABLE SAWHORSES (PAGE 60)

SIMPLE SAW GUIDE, WORK BENCH, END TABLE, A-FRAME MAILBOX (PAGES 63, 106, 102 AND 88)

BLUEBIRD HOUSE, HERB RACK, PICKET PLANTER, BIRD FEEDER (PAGES 120, 112, 115 AND 125)

SCANDINAVIAN SINGLE BED, UNDER-BED STORAGE BOX (PAGES 134 AND 79)

OPEN SHELVES (PAGE 93)

HEADBOARD WITH STORAGE, SIMPLE SHELF WITH PEGS, TOY CHEST, LETTER BOX (PAGES 129, 98, 84 AND 75)

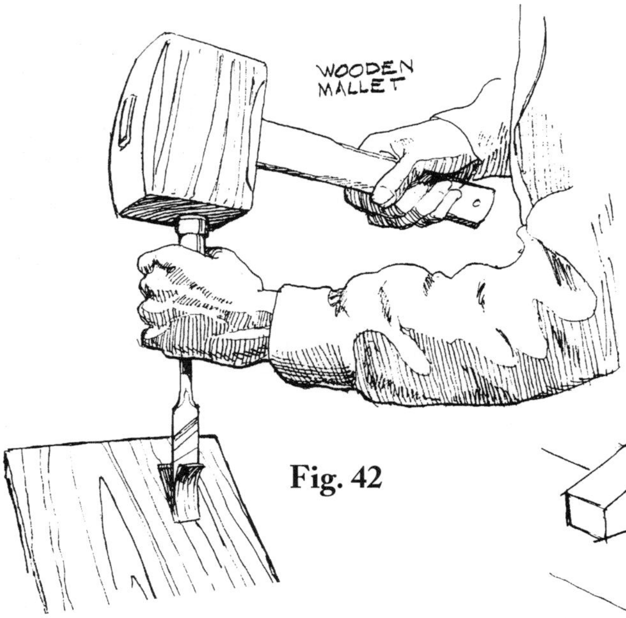

WOODEN MALLET

Fig. 42

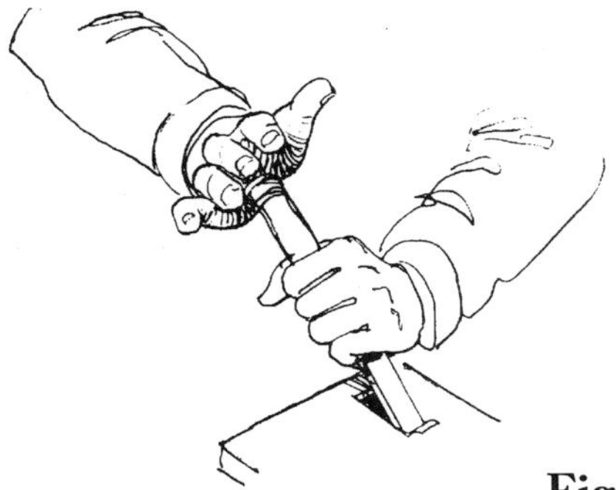

Fig. 43

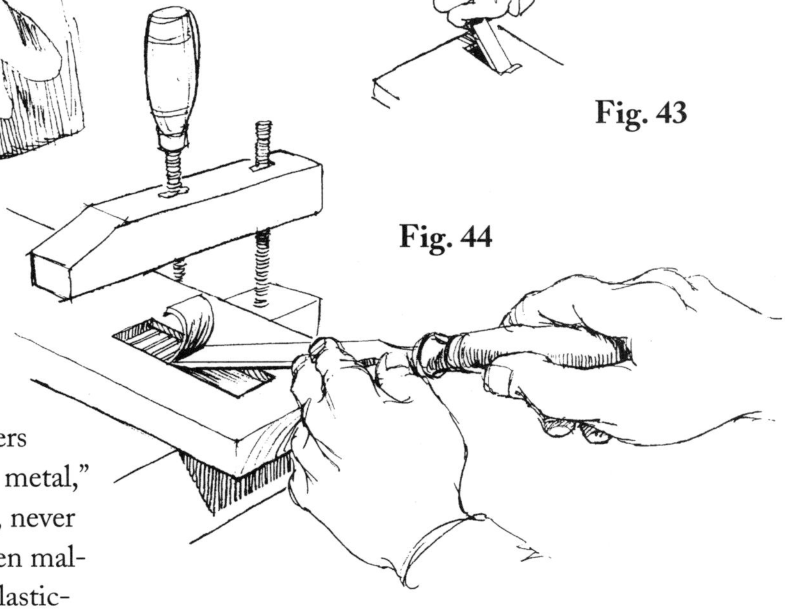

Fig. 44

One of the basic rules David remembers from shop class was "never hit wood with metal," so if you are using a wood-handled chisel, never hit it with a metal hammer—use a wooden mallet instead (see Fig. 42). A high-impact plastic-handled chisel, however, can be hit with either a wooden mallet or a metal hammer.

Much chiseling is done without a mallet or hammer, either by hitting it with the palm of your hand (see Fig. 43) or by using the weight of your body, as when you are "paring" (removing waste material in thin layers). Use wood clamps to hold the piece of wood that you are chiseling securely to a work table (see Fig. 44), and never put your hand in front of the chisel (see Fig. 45).

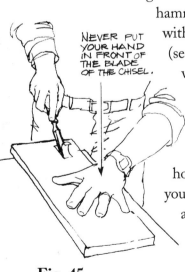

NEVER PUT YOUR HAND IN FRONT OF THE BLADE OF THE CHISEL.

Fig. 45

One of the most typical uses for a chisel is cutting out a groove, or "mortise," for hardware, such as a door hinge or a cabinet door pull. To do this, use a pencil to mark the shape of the groove. Holding the chisel in a vertical position with the beveled side of the chisel facing into the groove, tap the chisel with a mallet to make cuts approximately ⅛ inch deep around the outline of the groove (see Fig. 46). Next, holding the chisel in the same vertical position, make a series of parallel cuts, ⅛ inch apart and ⅛ inch deep, *inside* the groove. Chip out the excess wood in the groove either by holding the chisel almost parallel to the wood and lightly tapping the end of the handle with the palm of your hand (see Fig. 43) or by holding the handle with two hands and moving

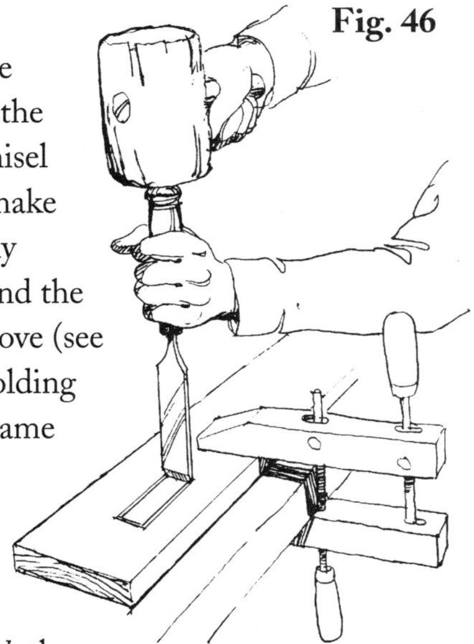

Fig. 46

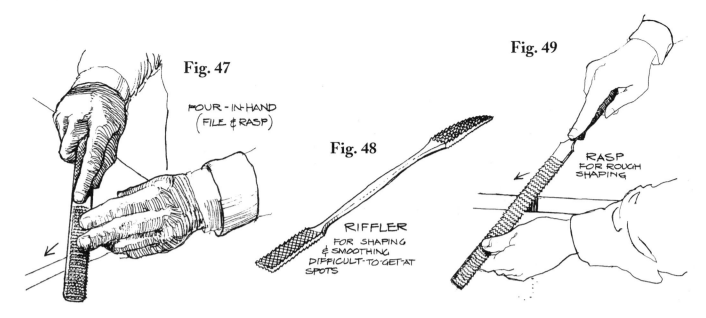

Fig. 47

FOUR-IN-HAND
(FILE & RASP)

Fig. 48

RIFFLER
FOR SHAPING
& SMOOTHING
DIFFICULT-TO-GET-AT
SPOTS

Fig. 49

RASP
FOR ROUGH
SHAPING

the bevel carefully through the groove (see Fig. 44). For a deeper groove, repeat the same process.

FILES AND RASPS

(see Figs. 47 through 49)

Although you may not need one often, there are times when you can't do without a good file or rasp. These tools are generally used when there is not enough wood to remove with a saw, but there's too much to remove using only sandpaper. When the edge of a board doesn't line up correctly with another board, for instance, it can be shaved down using a rasp or file.

Basically, the difference between a rasp and a file is that a rasp has larger, more aggressive teeth and is used more for shaping wood. A file, with its smaller and finer teeth, is for smoothing wood.

Files and rasps are fairly inexpensive, and a set of 12 different ones generally costs less than $9. If you prefer to start out with only one shaping tool, we recommend a "four-in-hand" (shoe) rasp, which has both coarse and fine teeth. It has file and rasp teeth on both sides (see Fig. 47). As you become a more proficient carpenter, a set of six rifflers makes an excellent investment, as these tools are perfect for getting into small corners (see Fig. 48).

Files and rasps generally come without handles; however, wooden handles are sold separately and can be fitted to your individual tool.

To use a file or rasp, securely clamp the piece to be filed to a work surface. Grasp the tool with two hands, one on the handle and the other on the point, guiding the tool. Use a downward pressure to force the teeth of the tool into the wood. Too little pressure causes the tool to catch on the wood grain, resulting in a rougher surface.

Always file across the work at an angle to avoid leaving ragged, overly rough surfaces (see Fig. 49). And remember, files and rasps are made to cut on the "push" stroke only. Lift the tool and bring it back into position before beginning the next stroke.

Fastening

FOR EVERY construction project you tackle, you will have to decide what type of fastener should be used to join the building materials together: nails, screws, bolts or glue. The most common fastener is a nail, which, of course, requires a hammer to drive it into the wood.

HAMMERS

(see Fig. 50)

When buying a hammer, there are some essential points to keep in mind: price, use, weight and handle composition. A good all-purpose hammer costs under $20. Cheap hammers are a bad investment, not only because they often result in bent nails, but also because the hammer head is more likely to chip, sending fragments of metal flying.

The most common, practical hammer for woodworking projects is the claw hammer, which comes in weights ranging from 7 ounces to 20 ounces. A 7-ounce hammer is useful when hammering small nails or brads. It is also a good hammer for a child to use. The 13-ounce size is a solid-weighted hammer that will do most jobs without being overly heavy. We like the Stanley Graphite 13-ounce curved claw hammer, model 51-440 (available at most hardware stores) because of its easy-to-grip ridged rubber handle, which is less likely to slip out of your hand than a smooth wooden-handled hammer.

Choosing between hammers with a metal or a wooden (hickory) handle is really a personal decision. If you can borrow both types from friends, it might be best to get some hands-on practice before buying one or the other. We have never broken a metal-handled hammer, but several of our wooden-handled hammers have bit the dust! Some old-timers, however, swear by their wooden-handled hammers.

The two most common types of claw hammers are the curved claw hammer and the 16- to 20-ounce straight claw (framing) hammer (see Fig. 50). The straight claw hammer is used for heavy, rough work; the curved claw hammer is best suited for general carpentry. The curved claws can remove nails easier than the straight claw hammer, which is used for wedging apart

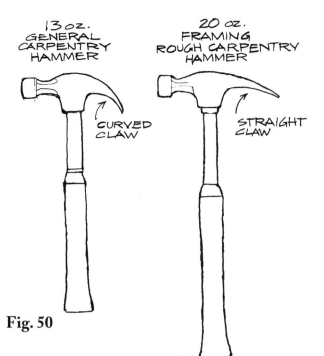

Fig. 50

boards, digging in the ground and rough salvage work. The claws on both hammers cannot draw a nail out of a board unless the nail head is sticking out at least ⅛ inch; therefore, it's a good idea to stop short of hammering nails all the way in until you are confident that everything fits together perfectly.

Most people start out using a hammer by gripping it halfway up the handle, close to the head (similar to "choking up" on the bat in baseball), instinctively feeling that this gives them more control (see Fig. 51). Choking up on the hammer *does* give you more control, which is useful when hammering small nails, but because there is less force in each blow, it requires more energy to finish hammering each nail.

Imagine that the hammer is an extension of your arm, and concentrate on keeping your wrist stiff. As you gain more confidence in carpentry, you will find that holding the hammer near the end of the handle leads to more efficient hammering (see Fig. 52). Improving your accuracy comes with practice, so find some scrap lumber and spend a little time driving nails into it.

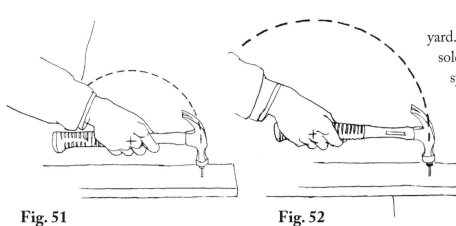

Fig. 51   **Fig. 52**

yard. Unfortunately, nails are often sold using the antiquated "penny" system, abbreviated as "d," which indicates the nail's length. (This and the "board foot" system of pricing lumber are slowly disappearing from use.) To help you identify nail sizes, refer to Fig. 53, which shows some common types drawn to scale.

NAILS

Nails are the quickest and most economical way to join two pieces of wood. They are usually sold in 1- and 5-pound boxes but can be bought more economically loose from bins at the lumber-

Hammering nails:

Nails can resist shear force; however, they can also easily and unexpectedly pull loose when nailed into the softer end grain of wood (see

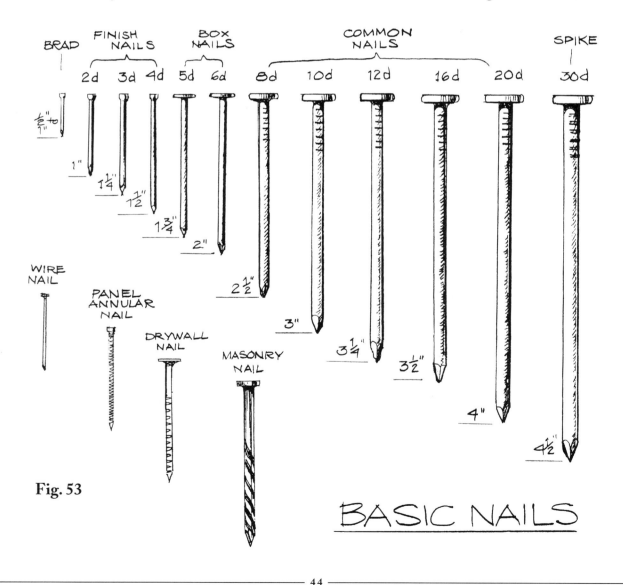

Fig. 53

BASIC NAILS

Fig. 54). When hammering nails into the end grain, use a longer nail than you would normally use to make sure that the nail is securely embedded in the wood.

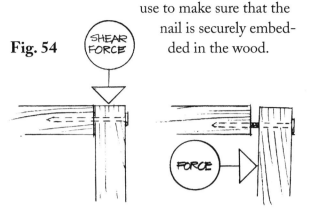

Fig. 54

If you are nailing short fine brads, such as those used on the back of a picture frame, you may find that your fingers are dangerously close to the head of the nail. To avoid hitting your fingers with the hammer, hold the nail with a pair of needle-nose pliers (see Fig. 55).

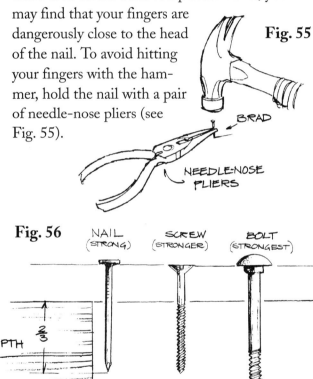

Fig. 55

BRAD

NEEDLE-NOSE PLIERS

Fig. 56

NAIL (STRONG)   SCREW (STRONGER)   BOLT (STRONGEST)

DEPTH $\frac{2}{3}$

Ideally, nails, screws and bolts should go completely through the first piece of wood and two-thirds of the way through the second piece of material you are nailing into (see Fig. 56).

Before you begin nailing, make sure the wood is centered over a very solid surface; otherwise,

the force of each blow will be reduced, making it more difficult to drive the nails. If you are working on a table, center the wood over one of the supporting table legs.

Start the nail by resting the hand holding the nail on the workpiece (see Fig. 57) and then giving the nail two or three light taps with the hammer until it remains upright in the wood without the support of your hand. As you hammer, keep your eye focused on the head of the nail. Try to direct your blows so that the nail is struck by the lower center face of the hammer head (see Fig. 58) and the handle of the hammer is parallel with the workpiece (see Fig. 59). There is more weight behind each blow this way, and you are less likely to miss the nail.

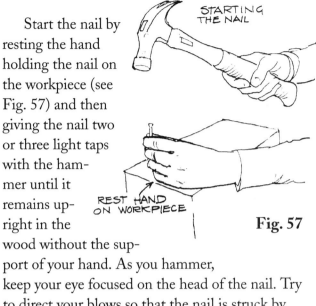

STARTING THE NAIL

REST HAND ON WORKPIECE

Fig. 57

STRIKE ZONE

Fig. 58

When you estimate that the nail is about to come through the underside of the first board, stop for a moment and look

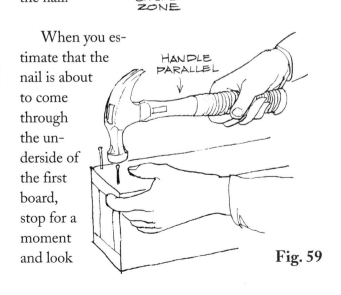

HANDLE PARALLEL

Fig. 59

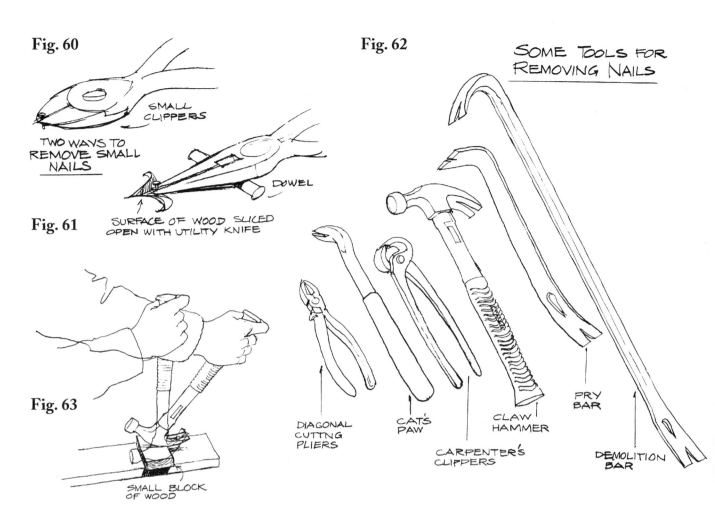

Fig. 60

SMALL CLIPPERS

TWO WAYS TO REMOVE SMALL NAILS

DOWEL

SURFACE OF WOOD SLICED OPEN WITH UTILITY KNIFE

Fig. 61

Fig. 63

SMALL BLOCK OF WOOD

Fig. 62

SOME TOOLS FOR REMOVING NAILS

DIAGONAL CUTTING PLIERS

CAT'S PAW

CARPENTER'S CLIPPERS

CLAW HAMMER

PRY BAR

DEMOLITION BAR

underneath to make sure that the two pieces you are joining are still lined up perfectly. You can even try feeling with your fingers to determine this. Because it is easy for the boards to shift slightly after the first blow of the hammer, it is important to check this early on; otherwise, you may pay dearly later. Once the boards are aligned perfectly, hold them together firmly with your other hand, or clamp them together, and give the nail a decisive blow, locking the two boards together in the correct position.

The last blow of the hammer is the most difficult, since it should be done with enough force to send the nail into the wood without denting the surface of the wood with the hammer head. This stroke takes practice to perfect. Once you have mastered it, it will become second nature to you and will improve the look of your carpentry.

Removing nails:

Removing nails is a science in itself, often requiring patience and forethought. If the nail is a small one, such as a 1-inch brad, it can be removed with a pair of small clippers, by levering the nail up, a bit at a time (see Fig. 60). If you need to remove a misaligned nail and its head is sunk in the wood, you may have to perform some minor surgery, cutting the wood out around the nail head so you can get a grip on it. If you are careful, you can split, but not remove, the wood around the nail head and lift the offending nail out using needle-nose pliers that are placed on a small dowel for leverage (see Fig. 61).

For removing medium-sized nails, a pair of carpenter's clippers (see Fig. 62) can be used without doing too much damage to the wood. If you are removing a particularly long nail, you may find it impossible to do unless you place a small block of wood under the hammer head to provide more leverage (see Fig. 63). Also, when removing nails from softwoods such as pine, cedar or redwood, the hammer head is likely to leave a dent unless a scrap of flat wood is first put under the hammer head.

For removing large nails (3 inches and larger), a special tool called a "cat's paw" (see Fig. 62) is hammered into the wood under the nail head and used to lift the nail head out.

If you don't have clippers or a cat's paw, use the claws on your hammer. You must, however, first lift the nail heads up so that you can get a grip on them. Do this by hammering a scrap piece of wood against one of the two nailed boards until they begin to separate (see Fig. 64). Tap the pointed end of the nails (on the bottom side of the board), so that the nail heads protrude out the other side of the board far enough to get a grip on them (see Fig. 65).

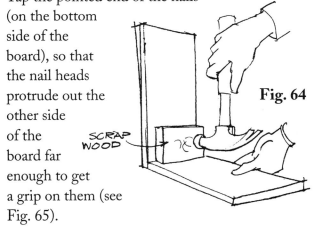

Fig. 64

SCRAP WOOD

Even the best carpenters are known to bend nails at times. If this happens to you, remove the nail and start over with a new one rather than try to straighten the old one. It doesn't pay to reuse a bent nail, since nails cost as little as three for one penny.

Fig. 65

Sometimes a nail will hit a knot in the wood. Once you feel resistance, stop hammering immediately, since removing a nail deeply embedded in a knot can be quite difficult. When you do encounter a knot, you have two choices: Either remove the nail and drill a pilot hole through the knot, or remove the nail and reposition it in a different spot.

SCREWS AND BOLTS

Most of the projects in this book are assembled using either nails or screws. For holding power, screws are far stronger than nails because the screw threads bite into the material surrounding the screw hole. Another advantage to using screws instead of nails is that they can be removed easily if things don't fit together perfectly—which is often the case. Screws come in different lengths, ranging from ¼ inch to 4 inches, as well as in different thicknesses or sizes, ranging from #0 to #24 gauge, which translates into 1/16 inch to ⅜ inch. The most commonly used screws for woodworking are #4, #6, #8, #10 and #12 gauge (see Fig. 66).

In general, the thicker the screw for a given length, the more substantial the holding power. A good rule of thumb is to use #4 screws when screwing into wood that is ½ inch thick, #6 or #8 screws for wood ¾ inch thick and #10 or #12 screws for wood 1½ inches thick. Wood that is thicker than 1½ inches is generally joined together using lag screws or bolts (see p. 51, Figs. 72 through 74).

The size of the screw also depends on the task. For instance, #4s are used primarily for very lightly stressed assemblies, such as crafts, small boxes, dollhouses or hinges; #6s have similar light-duty applications but can also be used for more robust stress levels, such as toys, children's furniture and drawer slides; #8s are the most common all-purpose screws and are often used for cabinets, furniture, doors, benches and other light construction; #10s are used for general construction and outdoor projects, such as decks, boat building, lawn furniture and more heavy-duty furniture; and #12s are used as heavy-duty construction fasteners for hanging heavy solid-core doors on sheds or barns, as well as for rough framing.

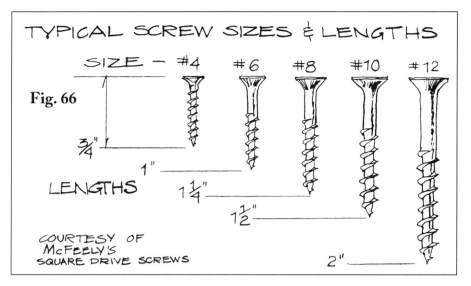

TYPICAL SCREW SIZES & LENGTHS

SIZE — #4   #6   #8   #10   #12

Fig. 66

LENGTHS

3/4"
1"
1 1/4"
1 1/2"
2"

COURTESY OF
McFEELY'S
SQUARE DRIVE SCREWS

Whenever possible, use a screw that is two to three times as long as the thickness of the wood into which you are screwing (see p. 45, Fig. 56). Screws or nails going into the end grain of another piece of wood should be even longer, since end-grain wood has less holding power than the flat or edge grain. When fastening woods of varying thicknesses, screw through the thinner and into the thicker piece of wood.

TYPES OF SCREWS

(see Fig. 67)

Slotted Screws (Roundhead and Flathead)

This type of screw is becoming less popular today because extreme twisting pressure when screwing into hardwoods can strip the screw head. The screwdriver can also easily slip off the screw head and put a severe gash in your finished work.

Phillips-Head Screws (Flathead)

The head of this screw has a "cross-slot" recess that helps keep the screwdriver from slipping off the screw head. This screw, which grew in demand after World War II, comes in a variety of sizes and configurations. Some Phillips-head screws are galvanized and good for outdoor use (for decks and garden structures, for instance). The charcoal-colored #6 drywall screws are often

used for installing drywall, but they can also be used for wood construction.

Square Drive Screws

Developed in 1908 by P. L. Robertson, a Canadian industrialist, these screws are used extensively in Canada, and now they're finding a growing market in the United States as well. They are easier to screw into wood than Phillips-head screws because the screwdriver is less likely to slip ("cam") out of the square hole in the screw head.

Drilling screws:

The process of drilling screws into wood has been much improved by the advent of the screw gun, which is basically a VSR electric drill with a screwdriver bit attachment. Using this tool makes drilling screws so much easier than screwing them in by hand that you might just as well forget about your old single-slotted screwdriver. To prevent overdrilling and stripping the screws, buy a cordless electric screwdriver with a clutch. Both Panasonic and DeWalt make good ones.

Making pilot holes:

Pilot holes are drilled into wood for two reasons: The first is to facilitate the drilling of the screw. The second, and less obvious reason, is the

Fig. 67

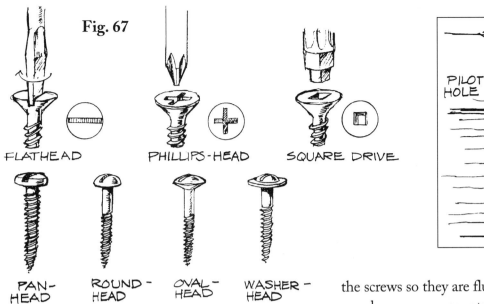

FLATHEAD   PHILLIPS-HEAD   SQUARE DRIVE

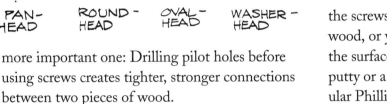

PAN-HEAD   ROUND-HEAD   OVAL-HEAD   WASHER-HEAD

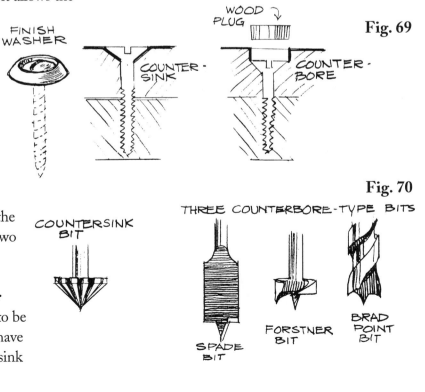

Fig. 68

PILOT HOLE   1ST BOARD   2ND BOARD

more important one: Drilling pilot holes before using screws creates tighter, stronger connections between two pieces of wood.

To understand this, think of the screw as a clamp. When screwing two boards together, the threads on the bottom part of the screw pull the bottom board tightly against the top board. Because a pilot hole is slightly larger in diameter than the threaded part of the screw, it allows the screw to slip easily through the first piece of wood and bite into the second piece of wood, clamping the two pieces together firmly (see Fig. 68). If pilot holes are not used, the screw threads can actually work against you. When drilling several screws into a piece of wood, for example, you may find that if the first screw is not drilled and held tightly, it prevents the rest of the screws from pulling the two pieces of wood together.

Countersinking and counterboring:
If you do not want screw heads to be above the surface of the wood, you have two choices: You can either countersink

the screws so they are flush with the surface of the wood, or you can counterbore the screws below the surface and fill the recessed area with wood putty or a wooden plug (see Fig. 69). Even a regular Phillips screwdriver can be used to slightly sink the head of a screw; however, this can create a splintery hole that is not as neat as you might wish. It is much more professional-looking to use a countersink or a counterbore bit and to finish off the job properly. Both bits fit into an electric drill and are quick and easy to use (see Fig. 70).

Fig. 69

FINISH WASHER   WOOD PLUG   COUNTER-SINK   COUNTER-BORE

Fig. 70

COUNTERSINK BIT   THREE COUNTERBORE-TYPE BITS   SPADE BIT   FORSTNER BIT   BRAD POINT BIT

Drilling a screw using an electric drill with a screwdriver bit (see Fig. 71):

1. Whenever possible, clamp the two pieces of wood together firmly, using a wooden clamp.

2. Decide how you want the screw to look, and drill either a countersunk or a counterbored "pilot" hole through the first board.

3. Choose the correct-sized screw and corresponding screwdriver drill bit.

4. Place the bit in the opening in the head of the screw.

5. Holding the drill firmly with two hands, check to make sure the drill is vertically over ("on axis" with) the screw head.

6. Squeeze the trigger slowly and drill until the screw head almost touches the wood.

7. Release the pressure on the trigger so that momentum carries the last twist of the screw, embedding the screw head into the wood. If you don't have a clutch on your drill and you don't stop the drill soon enough, you run the risk of "spinning" the screw in the hole, possibly stripping the wood or in some cases even snapping off the screw head.

8. Practice on scrap wood before starting a project.

WHEN DRILLING SCREWS, KEEP YOUR BODY WEIGHT DIRECTLY OVER THE SCREW AND KEEP YOUR HEAD IN FRONT SO YOU CAN SEE THE SCREW GOING IN.

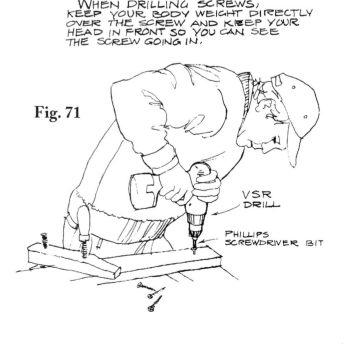

Fig. 71

VSR DRILL

PHILLIPS SCREWDRIVER BIT

There are two forces involved in drilling a screw: the downward force of the screwdriver on the screw head, and the twisting (torque) force of the drill and screw. If you let up on the downward force before the screw is driven all the way in, the drill is likely to "cam" or jump out of the screw-head slot.

CAUTION: 1. If you remove a long screw using the reverse gear on an electric drill, be careful about touching the screw with your bare hand, as it may have become very hot from the friction caused by the removal. **2.** Drywall and deck screws have very sharp points and may scratch or poke you if you put them in your pocket.

TIP: For very hard woods, coating the screws with wax—not soap—can make it easier to screw them into the wood. Soap can pull moisture out of the wood onto the screw, causing it to rust.

For hard-to-reach places (where it would be impossible to fit two hands), try fitting the screw onto the end of the screwdriver bit before screwing it into the wood, enabling you to work with only one hand in the space.

LAG SCREWS
(also called Lag Bolts)

Lag screws (see Fig. 72) are larger than regular screws. The most common sizes are ¼ inch to ½ inch in diameter and vary in length from 1 inch to 12 inches. When attaching two pieces of wood using a lag screw, drill a hole slightly larger in diameter than the lag screw through the first board. Drill a second pilot hole, slightly smaller in diameter than the lag screw, one-quarter of the way through the second board. Put a washer on the lag screw before inserting the lag screw through the hole in the first board and into the hole in the second board. Tap the head of the lag screw with a hammer and turn the hexagonal

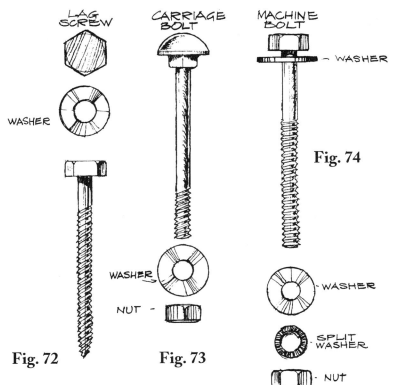

LAG SCREW

WASHER

Fig. 72

CARRIAGE BOLT

WASHER →

NUT -

Fig. 73

MACHINE BOLT

- WASHER

Fig. 74

- WASHER

- SPLIT WASHER

- NUT

The two most commonly used bolts are the carriage bolt (see Fig. 73) and the machine bolt (see Fig. 74). A carriage bolt has a round head with a shoulder that must be tapped into the wood before tightening the nut. It requires only one washer inside the nut at the end of the bolt.

A machine bolt has a hexagonal head and requires two wrenches to install: one to hold the bottom nut while the other wrench tightens the head. Machine bolts generally require a washer at both ends.

Bolts can be tightened periodically if the wood shrinks.

CLAMPS

(see Figs. 75 through 77)

One of the most worthwhile, and often overlooked, tools for woodworking is a clamp. It's difficult to glue two pieces of wood together perfectly without using clamps. Clamping the wood that you are working with also enables you to have both hands free.

Professional carpenters may have as many as 50 clamps in their shop. There are numerous types and shapes, the most common of which include the hand-screw wood clamp, pipe clamp, bar clamp, C-clamp and spring clamp (see Fig. 75). Our favorite is the Jorgensen hand-screw clamp because the "jaws" are made of wood and won't dent your work. Unlike most other clamps, it also has the advantage of being able to clamp pieces of wood at an angle (see Fig. 76). Another nice feature is that it can be released using only one hand.

When David first started using these clamps as a boy, he turned each handle, one at a time,

head a quarter turn, using a vise grip or wrench. Repeat this process until you feel the lag screw bite into the board. Continue turning the screw with the wrench until the washer is pressing into the surface of the wood of the first board.

BOLTS

(see Figs. 73 and 74)

Bolts are used in heavy construction, such as outdoor play equipment, porch railings and in situations where objects are going to be taken apart and reassembled. Just as screws have more holding power than nails, bolts have more holding power than screws. Nothing beats a bolt for strength.

A bolt has a straight, threaded shaft that is inserted into a predrilled hole the same diameter as the bolt and is fastened down with a washer and nut at its end. Bolts come in various lengths (¾ inch to 20 inches) and diameters (¼ inch to ¾ inch). The thicker the bolt, the stronger the fastener.

TYPES OF CLAMPS

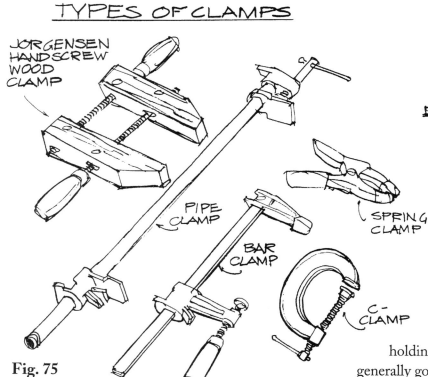

JORGENSEN HAND SCREW WOOD CLAMP

PIPE CLAMP

BAR CLAMP

SPRING CLAMP

C-CLAMP

Fig. 75

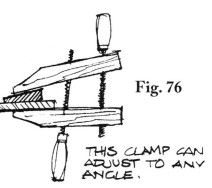

Fig. 76

THIS CLAMP CAN ADJUST TO ANY ANGLE.

while adjusting the distance between the jaws. This was very time-consuming! Years later, he was shown by his brother-in-law how to grasp both handles at the same time, rotating them in one direction or the other, thereby opening and closing the clamps much more quickly (see Fig. 77).

GLUES

Glue is often used to preassemble pieces of wood before nailing or screwing them together, which helps to keep them from slipping out of place. Joints that have been glued and clamped look more professional; they don't have unsightly gaps that require being filled with wood putty.

Over the past few years, glues have been improved and are now much stronger and more durable. For woodworking, yellow (carpenter's or wood) glue is

generally used. Many yellow glues, however, are not water-resistant. Titebond II bonds in a few minutes and, if applied according to directions, can become stronger than the wood it is holding. It is also water-resistant and generally good for outdoor building projects, as long as they are not exposed to constant water.

To get a really tight bond, always make sure that your wood pieces fit together well before gluing. Using a flat stick, cover the pieces where they are to be bonded with a light, even coat of glue. Clamp them together for an instant so that they become tacky. With a flat stick, spread out the glue and try to keep it away from the edges so that it won't ooze out from the sides. Press the pieces of wood together and shift them slightly. You should feel the pieces pull together. Clamp the pieces together while the glue is drying. Make sure to wipe off any excess glue immediately, using a damp sponge, as glue-smeared wood will not accept stain.

Fig. 77

TO ADJUST THE JORGENSEN WOOD CLAMP, GRASP THE TWO HANDLES AND ROTATE BOTH HANDS AT THE SAME TIME.

TIP: When gluing and clamping pieces of wood together, place a piece of waxed paper between the clamp jaw and the wood to prevent any glue from sticking to the jaws of the clamp. Also, adjust the jaws so they are holding the wood firmly but not too tightly.

Don't expect glue to fill gaps or uneven wood. Instead, use wood filler or sand the wood evenly. Glue will seep into the end grain of wood very quickly. If the wood does not look "wet" after applying a first coat, give it a second coat to ensure a good bond.

If the clamps you have are too large for a small project or if you don't have any clamps available, use rope, cord or tape to temporarily hold the pieces together after they have been glued.

CAUTION: Do not let glue freeze, as this causes it to become "gummy" and lose its strength. Never apply any type of yellow glue if the temperature is below 55 degrees F.

Sanding & Finishing

THE LAST STEP of any woodworking job is, in some respects, the most important. This is the time to correct any minor mistakes or imperfections by giving your building project a thorough sanding and finishing. Although sanding can be one of the most boring parts of carpentry, it is a crucial last step. Nothing creates a more professional, finished look than a smooth, careful sanding.

SANDPAPER

Sandpaper comes in 9x11 sheets or belts and is available in several grits ranging from coarse to medium to fine, calibrated in numbers. Generally speaking, 36-grit refers to very coarse, 40- to 50-grit refers to coarse, 60- to 100-grit refers to

medium, 120- to 220-grit refers to fine, and 240-grit and higher refers to extra-fine. (The larger the number, the smaller the grit size.) Sandpaper grit grades are listed on the back of each piece of sandpaper. Coarse sandpaper is used more for shaping, fine sandpaper for smoothing wood surfaces.

SANDING SAVVY

Important points to remember when sanding:
• Begin with a coarse sandpaper, such as 40-grit, in order to remove uneven surfaces and to clean up any joints that don't line up perfectly.
• Change to a medium-grade sandpaper such as 60-grit to further level and smooth the wood surface.
• Finish sanding, using a fine sandpaper such as 120- or 220-grit until the surface of the wood is soft and as smooth as satin.
• *Always* use a sanding block when sanding flat surfaces. If you don't, the result will be irregular shallow valleys in the wood that will show up when a glossy finish is applied.

You can make a sanding block out of a scrap piece of 1x4 or 1x3. Cut a sheet of sandpaper in half by placing it (rough side down) on a flat table, laying a steel straightedge or ruler on top and ripping the sandpaper against the straightedge (see Fig. 78). Fold the sandpaper over the block of wood (see Fig. 79), and hold the paper in place with your hand as you sand, using long, even strokes moving along the grain of the wood.

End grain can be sanded in any direction. When sanding uneven or contoured surfaces, such as moldings, use a foam sanding pad or foam sanding block for best results.

To sand in tight corners, use a full sheet of sandpaper folded into eighths; to sand the inside of holes, curl sandpaper into a tight roll or make a sanding stick by wrapping a piece of sandpaper around a wooden dowel (see Fig. 79).

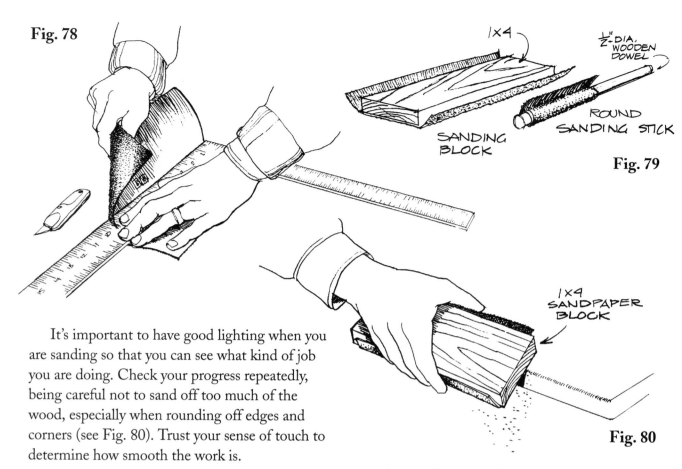

Fig. 78

Fig. 79

SANDING BLOCK

1x4

½"-DIA. WOODEN DOWEL

ROUND SANDING STICK

1x4 SANDPAPER BLOCK

Fig. 80

It's important to have good lighting when you are sanding so that you can see what kind of job you are doing. Check your progress repeatedly, being careful not to sand off too much of the wood, especially when rounding off edges and corners (see Fig. 80). Trust your sense of touch to determine how smooth the work is.

Sharp corners and edges often look and "feel" better if they are rounded off slightly. Most house builders know that if you round off the corner edges slightly, paint is less likely to crack. Even if you own the latest and most expensive sanding machinery, the smoothest finish is achieved by giving your project a final hand sanding.

POWER SANDERS

To be perfectly honest, sanding can get boring, especially if you have large surfaces to cover. Power sanders, however, can help speed up the sanding process.

Electric Palm Sander

(see Fig. 81)

This is a great sander for most of the projects in this book, and a good one can be bought for under $50 (we use a Porter-Cable). The advantages of this sander are that it sands flat, without

any chance of gouging the surface of the wood; it is lightweight, relatively quiet and easy to operate; and it uses only a quarter of a 9x11-inch sheet of sandpaper. The only disadvantage, if you can call it that, is that a palm sander does not remove a lot of material in a short time.

Random Orbit Sander

(see Fig. 82)

For a tool that can cover a larger area, the next step up is a random orbit sander. Most of these sanders come with replaceable self-adhering sandpaper with holes in it, enabling the sandpaper dust to be sucked up into a canister that can be removed and emptied. The face of the random orbit sander spins in a circular, orbital motion. A useful feature found on the Ryobi model Y115, which costs around $70, is that the speed of the sander can be adjusted. This type of sander is a vast improvement over the standard circular 4-inch disk pads that run off an electric drill.

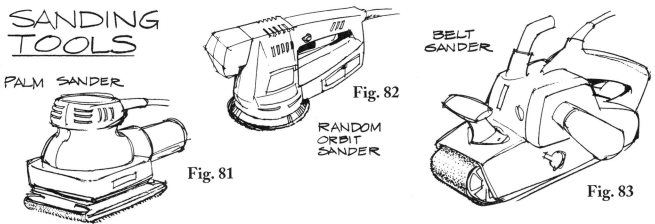

SANDING TOOLS

PALM SANDER

Fig. 81

Fig. 82

RANDOM ORBIT SANDER

BELT SANDER

Fig. 83

Belt Sander
(see Fig. 83)

This heavy-duty, expensive sander is useful if you need to sand several long boards. It is an aggressive machine and can run away from you if you don't keep a firm grip on it. Porter-Cable came out with the first belt sander in 1926, and the company still makes one of the best products—model PC00352, costing around $165. Nothing beats this sander for removing material in a hurry, especially if you use it with a coarse sanding belt.

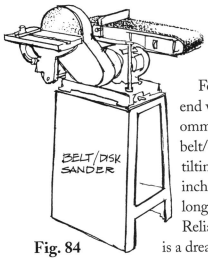

BELT/DISK SANDER

Fig. 84

Stationary Belt/ Disk Sander
(see Fig. 84)

For the serious weekend woodworker, we recommend a stationary belt/disk sander with a tilting table and large (6 inches wide by 24 inches long) sanding surface. Reliant makes one that is a dream machine!

FINISHING & FINISHES

After rough-sanding your project with 60-grit sandpaper, use a nail set to hammer the finish nails below the surface. Never substitute a blunt nail for this tool—it seldom works, and it can

skid off the nail you are sinking, resulting in additional holes or dents in the wood. Hold the nail set directly over the nail, and sink it with one or two sharp blows of the hammer (see Fig. 85).

The nail set leaves a 1/16-inch hole, which should be filled with wood putty. If you are working with white pine, we recommend using Durham's Water Putty (available at most hardware stores). It dries the same color as the wood and can be easily sanded smooth. It comes in powder form

Fig. 85

NAIL SET

REST YOUR LITTLE FINGER ON THE SURFACE OF THE WOOD TO HELP STEADY YOUR HAND WHILE SETTING THE NAIL.

and is mixed with an amazingly small amount of water (3 parts powder to 1 part water). It can easily be applied using a small spackling knife, rubber spatula or even a recycled popsicle stick. After filling the nail holes, wait 15 minutes, then sand the surface smooth using 120-grit sandpaper.

If you are building a project with a darker wood, use Plastic Wood, which comes in several colors, to fill the holes. Plastic Wood does not have to be mixed. It comes in tubes or cans and is either squeezed out or applied using a small knife or stick. If Plastic Wood is not available in the color you need, after filling the nail hole use oil paints to match the color of the wood, painting over the blemish with a small brush.

For wood projects that are going to be used outside, and may actually look better weathered, you may want to leave them in their natural state. Most projects, however, benefit from having a protective finish of some kind to help keep them clean and to protect them from moisture.

CAUTION: Before applying any finishes to wood, carefully read the directions and warnings on the label. Many finishes are combustible and have toxic vapors. Always wear protective rubber gloves when applying finishes.

Although wood can be painted, you can show off your craftsmanship by simply applying a coat of protective oil such as Thompson's Waterseal after you have sanded the wood. This is a transparent penetrating waterproofer that creates a moisture barrier on the surface of the wood. Before you start, make sure that the wood's surface is completely clean and dry, so that the oil can penetrate the wood evenly and thoroughly. Test a small amount first on a piece of scrap wood, then in a well-ventilated work space, apply the oil liberally with a brush. After 15 minutes, go over the surface again with a brush or cloth to eliminate any puddles.

Stains can also be applied to wood either to make it look like a different type of wood or to appear weathered. Most stains, however, are not waterproof or wearproof and should be covered with a protective finish.

Another finishing choice is tung oil, which resists moisture and mildew and leaves wood with a natural-looking, durable finish. It's available in both high and low gloss. Formsby's makes a good tung oil that dries clear, showing off the natural wood grain. Apply a small amount using a soft, clean cotton cloth and rub it thoroughly into the wood. Allow the wood to dry completely, then buff it lightly with a piece of fine steel wool. Wipe the surface clean, using a dry cloth, and apply a second coat. For projects that will receive wear and tear, like children's furniture, another option is to cover the wood with two coats of polyurethane. Allow the initial coat to dry thoroughly, then lightly sand it with fine steel wool. Wipe the surface clean with a soft cloth and apply a second coat.

A new product that we have used successfully is Varathane's Elite Diamond Finish, which comes in clear satin, gloss or semi-gloss. This is a nonyellowing, odorless, fast-drying, durable finish. Since this product is water-based, it is also easy to clean up, and it's one of the few products that is nontoxic and has very little odor. It appears milky when wet, but dries to a transparent finish. Stir it often but don't shake it. Don't use it if the temperature is below 50 degrees F. Because Varathane's Elite Diamond Finish is fast-drying, it should be brushed on quickly. Although it appears to dry immediately, allow two hours before applying a second coat. Sand the finish lightly using a very fine (220-grit) sandpaper, *not* steel wool, and clean the surface with a dry, soft cloth before applying another coat.

Another alternative, which results in a natural-looking finish that shows off a smooth sanding job, is to apply a couple of coats of wax to the surface of the wood. We use natural Briwax, an expensive but good wax polish, available in most hardware and paint stores. Apply a small amount with a clean cloth, rubbing the wax in with the grain of the wood. After wiping off any excess wax, buff the surface until it has a natural glow. Repeat the process one or two more times, until the wood has a rich luster.

Woodworking
PROJECTS

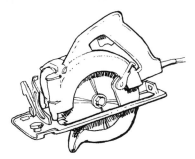

THE FIRST FOUR PROJECTS in this book describe how to build sawhorses, a saw guide, a nail box and a toolbox. Having a strong and stable work surface, an easy way to make perfect cuts, and a place to store your tools and nails are basic ingredients for success with any carpentry project.

The second group of projects concentrates on boxes of various sizes and shapes. Before beginning a box project, read "Building Boxes" (see p. 58), which contains general information on box construction. Once you have built a box successfully, you should be able to build any of the other projects in this book.

The next four projects—for shelves and tables—are useful, practical designs that solve common storage problems. The pointers in "Building Shelves" (see p. 58) will help get you started. As you gain more confidence in your building skills, you can adapt these designs to different dimensions appropriate to your specific needs.

The portable herb rack, picket planter, bluebird house and bird feeder —all "outdoor" projects that can be constructed in less than three hours—are easy ways to enhance your garden with flowers, herbs and songbirds.

The last three projects are for beds, each designed for different needs. Although they are impressive-looking and may appear to be complicated, these beds are not difficult to construct.

Building Boxes

IF YOU HAVE NEVER BUILT anything out of wood, the best way to learn is by building a box. This isn't as easy as you think, however. There are many points to consider:

- How will the sides be joined together?
- How thick should the wood be?
- What type of fasteners should be used (nails, glue)?
- What tools do you need?
- How can you make perfect right-angle cuts?
- What finish, if any, should be used?

A box consists of five pieces of wood, all of which need to be planned, measured, cut to size, sanded, fastened together and given a final sanding and finish. If just one of the cuts is slightly off, it will be obvious when the project is completed. That's why the planning and measuring of the pieces before they are cut are so important.

Before building a box, you must first decide what you want it to hold. Measure and write down the length, width and height of the objects that you want the box to contain. Then design the box accordingly.

The grain of the wood generally runs horizontally around a box. The ends of the front and back pieces of the box overlap and hide the unattractive edges of the side pieces.

After cutting the pieces for the box, lay them out in place and label each lightly in pencil where it won't show. This makes identifying the pieces and assembling the box easier.

Building Shelves

OPEN SHELVES are one of the most useful, practical projects you can build, and they can be fairly simple to construct as long as you follow a few basic rules:

- Decide how the shelves will be used and where they will be placed before you buy any lumber. If they will hold books or decorative objects, you'll need to buy lumber that is wide enough to accommodate them. You also will want to vary the distance between the shelves, since the items will be of different heights. With this in mind, do a rough sketch of the project. Once you've come up with a design you like, draw a plan to scale (1 inch = 1 foot) on graph paper, and double-check your measurements.

- Remember that shelves can sag without adequate support. If you are using ¾-inch stock (such as 1x12s), make sure that you support the shelves every 3 feet to prevent them from bending in the middle under a heavy load. Or use 5⁄4-inch stock, which is thicker, stronger and more attractive than ¾-inch stock and can support spans up to 4 feet. When selecting your lumber, check it carefully so you don't buy cupped or warped boards.

- Most walls have a 4- to 6-inch-high baseboard. Don't forget to take this into consideration when planning your shelves. You may have to notch out a small section of wood on the back of the shelf supports to allow space for this molding.

- Floors are rarely perfectly flat. Check them, using a level and a square, and trim off the bottom of the shelf uprights if necessary.

- If the shelves are going to be higher than 3 feet, attach them to the wall with 3-inch #10 drywall screws or drywall anchors so they cannot be pulled over accidentally (see p. 97, Fig. 10).

• If you are renting your house or apartment, you may want to design shelves that can be disassembled, so that you can take them with you if you move.

• The type of wood you use for shelves depends on whether or not you are going to paint them. If you are, #2 common 1x10s or 1x12s are fine. Fill any holes or knots with Plastic Wood or a water-based wood putty. Sand all the wood and give it a primer coat, using a roller, before assembling. Remember that knots in #2 common lumber can bleed through paint, so be sure to use a good shellac-based sealer.

If you are not painting your shelves, the best wood to buy is ⁵⁄₄x8 or ⁵⁄₄x10 clear white pine stock. It is expensive but looks beautiful when sanded and covered with a light stain. Two other less expensive alternatives are 2x8s or 2x10s— thicker, rougher lumber with a rustic appearance. It would require too much sanding to make this lumber practical to paint, but it is attractive stained a dark brown or ebony. This lumber measures 1½ inches thick and is able to take heavier loads than the ⁵⁄₄ stock, which actually measures about 1 inch.

Locating wall studs:

Most (but not all) houses built after World War II have studs spaced at 16-inch intervals on-center. To locate wall studs, measure from the nearest corner in 16-inch increments and mark where you think the studs should be. Pound the wall at these places with your fist and listen for the most solid sound.

To prevent the possibility of accidental shock, always turn off the electricity in that section of the house at the fuse box or circuit breaker. Next, drive a long nail into the wall where you think the stud should be. If it hits something solid and is difficult to remove, you've probably found the stud. If not, open up the hole a little and probe with a screwdriver or coat hanger to the left and right to see if you can feel the stud. Mark where you think the stud is and make another exploratory hole.

When you're sure you are dead center over the stud, measure over 16 inches (24 inches in some houses) and hammer in another nail. If you don't find a stud there, begin the same process over at the new location.

If you are apprehensive about punching holes in a nice, smooth wall, be assured that they can easily be patched with plaster spackle and paint. Spackle is sold wet or dry, and either form works well for all kinds of jobs. To use dry spackle, mix it with water to a putty- or doughlike consistency. (A rubber dust pan makes a great mixing container.) Using a 4-inch-wide flexible putty knife, a kitchen sandwich spreader or a spatula, fill the hole with spackle. After it has set for a few minutes, wipe it lightly with a flat, wet sponge. Wait until after the spot has thoroughly dried before sanding it with fine sandpaper wrapped around a block of wood (see p. 53-54 and Figs. 78 and 79). Repeat the process if there are any remaining depressions, then touch up the spackle spots using the same paint color as the rest of the wall.

Simple board shelving looks fine for a child's room or in a basement, but if you are making a more decorative piece for your living or dining room, glue and nail clear pine 1x2s to the front edges of the shelving. This will give the shelves a finished look as well as make them stronger and more substantial.

Adjustable

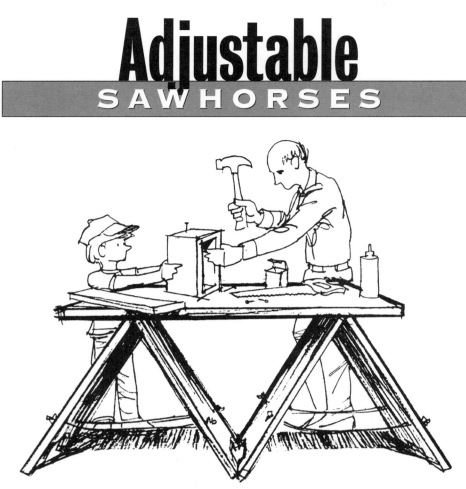

ONE OF THE MOST IMPORTANT yet overlooked items that a carpenter or woodworker needs is a solid support to rest his or her wood on while cutting it. Sawhorses can be bought for approximately $20 each; however, the ready-made ones are difficult to store, hard to transport and are not adjustable.

A better alternative is to build your own. Two inexpensive sawhorses can be made from a single sheet of plywood, with the leftover piece serving as a work surface or tabletop. They are adjustable and can be easily folded up and stored away when not in use.

The bottoms of each pair of folding plywood legs are connected with ropes so that the height of the sawhorses can be raised or lowered. The sawhorses can also be used as a support for a tabletop. We use ours on Thanksgiving, when we need more table space for guests.

Referring to the Cutting Plan (see Fig. 1), use a T-square or tape measure and a pencil to mark the sawhorse dimensions on the plywood. Rest the sheet of plywood on three 2x4s, laid on edge on the floor, and check to make sure there is enough room for the jigsaw blade to cut through the plywood without touching the floor. Clamp an 8-foot piece of a scrap 1x6 to the plywood to act as a straightedge while cutting (see p. 28, Fig. 34). Use an electric jigsaw or a portable circular saw (see p. 26, Fig. 28A and 28B) to cut four identical pieces, each measuring 24x36 inches, from a 4x8-foot sheet of exterior plywood. When joined together, these pieces form the legs of the sawhorses. The 24x48-inch leftover piece of plywood will serve as the tabletop.

MATERIALS LIST

Quantity	Size	Description	Location or Use
4	24x36 inches	¾-inch exterior plywood	leg supports
1	24x48 inches	¾-inch exterior plywood	tabletop
4	1x3-inch	butt hinges with screws	leg supports
1 sheet	9x11 inches	60-grit sandpaper	hand holds
1	14 feet	¼-inch-dia. rope	leg supports
4	2-inch	Phillips-head screws	tabletop

Fig. 1

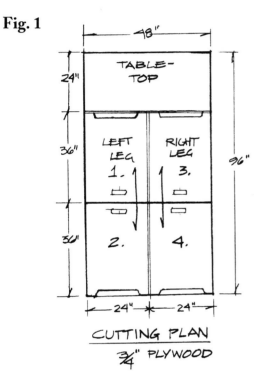

Fig. 2

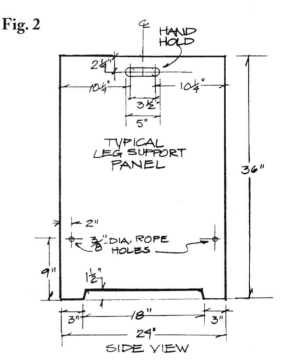

If you plan on using the sawhorses outside, cut out a 1½x18-inch section from the bottom of each panel (see Fig. 2, Side View) with an electric jigsaw. Begin and end the cuts 3 inches in from each side of the two 24x36-inch panels. Lay two panels (with the good side facing down) end to end and join them together, using 1x3-inch butt hinges placed 3 inches in from the outside edge of the plywood (see Fig. 3). When screwing the hinges onto the plywood, make sure that the pin of each hinge is centered between the two pieces of plywood. Repeat this procedure for the other two panels.

Optional: Hand holds can be cut from the top of each panel. Measure down 2¼ inches from the top and 10¼ inches from the sides of each panel and make two pencil marks to indicate where drill holes should be made. To prevent tear-out from the back of the wood (see p. 31), place a piece of scrap wood under the panel before you begin drilling your holes. Using a 1½-inch-diameter hole saw or a 1½-inch spade bit in a VSR electric drill (see p. 31, Fig. 40), bore two holes in each panel at the pencil marks. Use an electric jigsaw to cut out the section between each of the two holes, making an elongated slot (see

Fig. 3

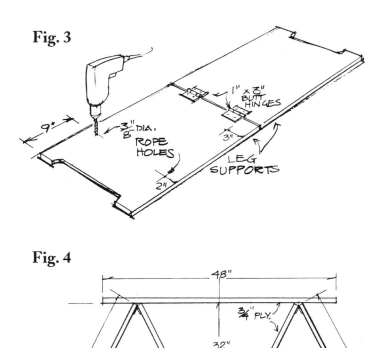

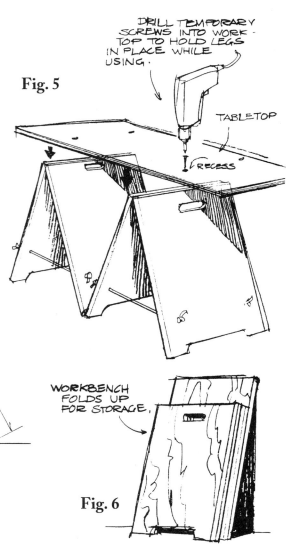

Fig. 4

Fig. 2). Smooth the inside edges of the hand holds with 60-grit sandpaper. **NOTE:** To keep the blade of the jigsaw from hitting the floor, rest the two panels on two 2x4s, placed on edge.

Drill two ⅜-inch-diameter rope holes, each 9 inches from the bottom and 2 inches from the side edges of each of the four panels (see Fig. 3).

Cut four pieces of ¼-inch-diameter rope, each 42 inches long. Stand each sawhorse up and thread the ends of the ropes through the holes (see Fig. 4), tying a knot at each end to keep the rope from pulling out. Adjust the knots so that the ropes are the same length when the legs are spread open. The distance between each pair of legs should be approximately 32 inches. Stand the two folding legs up so the bottom of two sides touch each other.

To make the tabletop, position the leftover piece of plywood over the two sawhorses. Using an electric drill with a Phillips screwdriver bit, drill four 2-inch screws through the tabletop and into the top edge of each sawhorse; there should be two screws on each side (see Fig. 5). **NOTE:** Make sure that the screws are countersunk, or recessed, below the surface of the plywood tabletop, so that they won't mar anything placed on top of the table (see p. 49, Fig. 69).

When the sawhorses are not in use, they can be easily disassembled. Use the same electric drill, in reverse, to remove the screws from the tabletop, and fold and store the pieces in a convenient place (see Fig. 6).

Simple
SAW GUIDE

MAKING ACCURATE right-angle crosscuts is important in every aspect of carpentry; therefore, we strongly suggest that before going on to any of the other projects, you build this simple device called a saw guide. It costs less than $10 for materials, takes less than an hour to construct and will greatly increase the accuracy of your cuts.

If you live in a small apartment, the saw guide can be used on a kitchen counter without marring it, and it can be conveniently stored away when not in use.

Although it may look new to you, this saw guide is actually a variation on the "bench hook,"

an age-old device used to hold wood securely while cutting it. We have improved it by adding two triangular pieces of wood, which not only make it easier to use but also enable you to make 45-degree miter cuts for picture frames and other projects. When we compared test cuts made with expensive power saws with those made with an inexpensive handsaw and this saw guide, we found that the handsaw cuts were consistently more accurate and smoother. Using the handsaw with the saw guide underneath it also prevents tear-out (see p. 31), which often results with an electric saw.

Our saw guide is also adjustable in case it gets out of alignment, and it takes only minutes to

MATERIALS LIST

Quantity	Size	Description	Location or Use
1	36 inches	1x10 #2 common pine	base & triangular guide pieces
1	26¾ inches	1x3 #2 common pine	fence
1	26¾ inches	1x2 #2 common pine	hook
10	1½-inch	#10 pan-head screws & washers	fence & triangular guide pieces
1 bottle	8 oz.	carpenter's glue	base, fence & hook

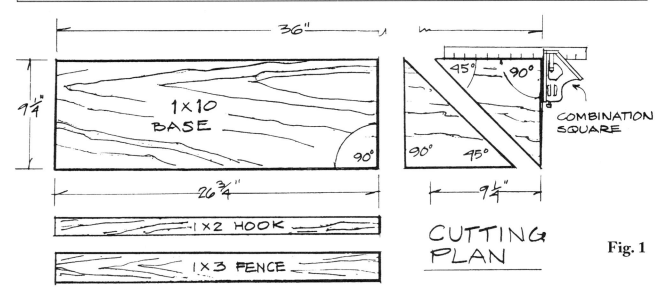

Fig. 1

change, whereas our notorious radial arm saw often requires an hour to realign. Although the saw guide is set up for ¾-inch-thick wood, it can be modified to accept 1½-inch-thick wood by adding another 1x3 to the fence and using longer screws.

When buying the materials at your lumberyard, ask one of the people working there to cut the 36-inch-long 1x10 into three pieces, using a radial arm saw and following the Cutting Plan (see Fig. 1). One piece, 26¾ inches long, will become the base piece, and the two triangular pieces will become the saw guide. This requires only two cuts: a 45-degree diagonal cut, and a 90-degree perpendicular cut. Check the angles of both cuts with a combination square to make sure

they are exact, for all future cuts will depend on these. The other two pieces of lumber, the 1x3 "fence" and the 1x2 "hook," should each be cut 26¾ inches long. The 1x3 should be perfectly straight, as it will be used as the "guide" for cutting lumber when the project is completed.

Place the base piece on top of a stable work surface. Lay a bead of carpenter's glue on the top surface of the hook, spreading it evenly with a flat stick. Using two wood clamps, attach the hook to the underneath front edge of the base piece (see Fig. 2). Make sure that the front and side edges of the two pieces are flush with each other. The hook is the part that rests against your workbench, counter or table (see illustration, p. 63).

HOW TO BUILD A SAW GUIDE

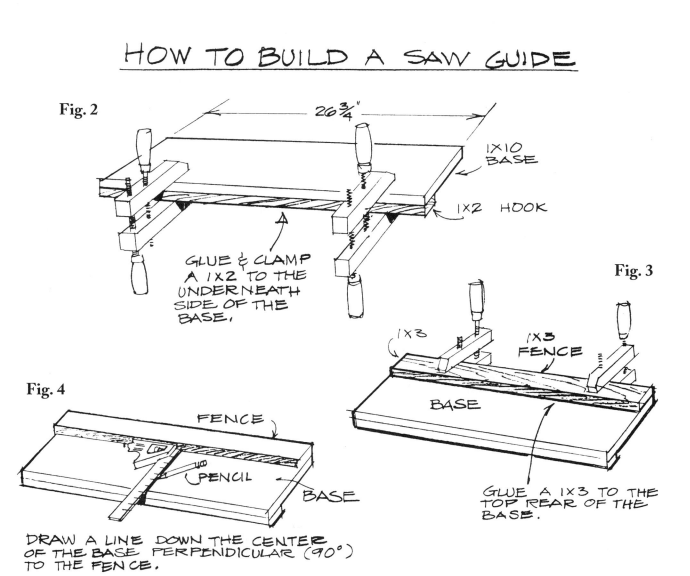

Fig. 2

26¾"

1X10 BASE

1X2 HOOK

GLUE & CLAMP A 1X2 TO THE UNDERNEATH SIDE OF THE BASE.

Fig. 3

1X3

1X3 FENCE

BASE

GLUE A 1X3 TO THE TOP REAR OF THE BASE.

Fig. 4

FENCE

PENCIL

BASE

DRAW A LINE DOWN THE CENTER OF THE BASE PERPENDICULAR (90°) TO THE FENCE.

When the glue has dried (approximately 45 minutes), glue and clamp the fence to the top rear of the base piece (see Fig. 3). Next, use a combination square and pencil to mark a line from the center of the base piece perpendicular to the fence (see Fig. 4). Double-check the accuracy of your line with the square.

Temporarily position the two triangular pieces of wood over the middle of the fence (see Fig. 5). Align them so that their back edges are flush with the back edge of the fence. **NOTE:** Make sure that the grain of the wood is running from front to rear, not sideways.

With a pencil, mark five screw locations on each triangle directly over the fence, as shown. Remove the triangles and, using an electric drill, bore ¼-inch-diameter (oversized) holes where the marks are, all the way through the triangles. Make sure that the right angles of the two triangular pieces are perpendicular to the fence (use the pencil line as a guide). Allow for a slight gap between the two triangles, exactly the same width as your saw blade. You can even use the saw as a spacer when you are attaching the triangles.

Screw the triangles down onto the fence with 1½-inch #10 pan-head screws and washers. We recommend attaching the triangles with screws,

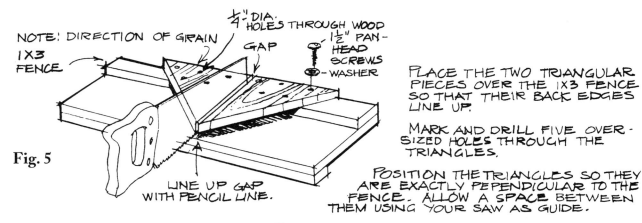

NOTE: DIRECTION OF GRAIN
1X3 FENCE
$\frac{1}{4}$" DIA. HOLES THROUGH WOOD
GAP
$1\frac{1}{2}$" PAN-HEAD SCREWS
WASHER

Fig. 5

LINE UP GAP WITH PENCIL LINE.

PLACE THE TWO TRIANGULAR PIECES OVER THE 1X3 FENCE SO THAT THEIR BACK EDGES LINE UP.

MARK AND DRILL FIVE OVER-SIZED HOLES THROUGH THE TRIANGLES.

POSITION THE TRIANGLES SO THEY ARE EXACTLY PEPENDICULAR TO THE FENCE. ALLOW A SPACE BETWEEN THEM USING YOUR SAW AS GUIDE.

SCREW THE TRIANGLES TO THE 1X3 FENCE USING TEN #10 $1\frac{1}{2}$" PAN-HEAD SCREWS AND WASHERS.

rather than glue, so that you have the option of adjusting the gap later on simply by loosening the screws and repositioning the triangles.

In order to place each new piece of wood correctly under the triangles, you will need an inspection hole to see where to cut. Use a 1-inch-diameter spade bit in a VSR electric drill to bore a hole through the triangles at a point where the saw slot intersects the fence (see Fig. 6). Before drilling this hole, place a piece of scrap wood under the spot where you will be drilling, so the drill bit will not cause tear-out on the underneath surface of the wood when exiting the triangles.

Test the accuracy of the saw guide by sliding and clamping a piece of scrap lumber under the triangles, flush against the fence. Carefully and slowly insert your saw in the saw slot (it should be tight at first) and saw through the scrap lumber (see Fig. 7). When sawing, the "power" stroke should be the forward stroke, moving away from your body. Keep checking as you saw to make

BORE A 1" DIA. INSPECTION HOLE WHERE THE TWO TRIANGLES INTERSECT THE FRONT EDGE OF THE FENCE.

SCRAP WOOD

Fig. 6

sure that the saw blade is positioned correctly and is not tilting to one side or the other or tipping too far forward or backward.

NOTE: It will be difficult at first to know when you have sawed through the scrap wood. Don't be fooled by the top of the saw, which is tapered down toward the tip. After several cuts, you'll be able to feel and hear a difference when the saw has gone through the wood. Don't be afraid to overcut slightly into the baseboard, as

Fig. 7

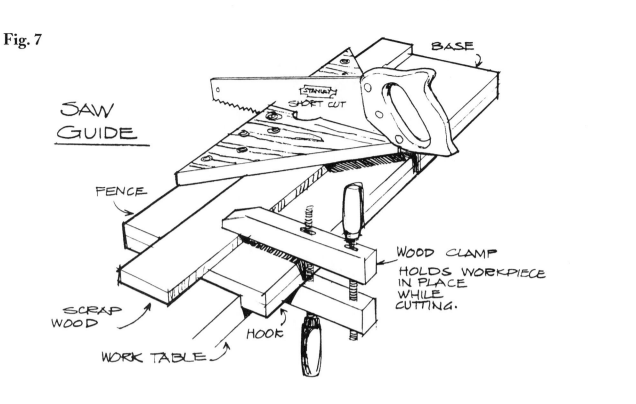

this will happen from time to time. Just don't overcut so much that you cut the whole saw guide board in half!

When you have finished the trial cut, remove the scrap wood and check to see if it was cut square. This is done by holding a combination square against the end of the wood (see Fig. 8). If it's not square, loosen the screws and adjust the triangles so they are properly aligned.

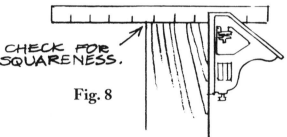

Fig. 8

NOTE: Always remove the sawdust from underneath the triangles before inserting the next piece of wood against the fence.

Nail

BOX

THIS SIMPLE NAIL BOX will come in handy when building just about anything, because every carpenter needs a place to store nails. It enables you to find your nails quickly and to carry them easily, instead of juggling two or three flimsy cardboard nail boxes.

Each compartment holds a large handful of nails. We stock ours with 1¼-inch, 1½-inch and 2-inch finish nails, which we use most often. In addition to being useful in the workshop, this box can serve as desktop storage for paper clips, rubber bands and other similar-sized office supplies.

Although this project is not difficult to build, it is essential that you make your cuts straight and square so the pieces fit together neatly. You might want to practice your cuts on scrap lumber first. Once you begin the box, take time to carefully measure and cut the seven pieces of wood.

Before beginning this project, look carefully at the Cutting Plan (see Fig. 1) and the other illustrations, and notice how all the pieces fit together.

The end pieces fit between the side pieces, and the bottom piece fits inside all four of the box sides. **NOTE:** The end pieces measure 3½ inches high and the two partition pieces measure 2¾ inches high; this is to allow for the ¾-inch thickness of the bottom (see Fig. 2).

The seven pieces that make up this nail box can all be cut from one 48-inch-long 1x4, including an allowance for the thickness (kerf) of the saw blade (approximately ⅛ inch) plus some additional waste.

Although we have suggested pine, any type of wood can be used—even scrap wood. All of the pieces can be easily and accurately cut with a handsaw and saw guide (see p. 63), but if you don't have a saw guide, use an electric jigsaw with a speed square as a guide (see p. 27, Fig. 30).

Clamp the 1x4 board to your worktable, and then check to make sure it has square ends. If not, mark each one with a speed square or combination square and cut them off squarely. Next, care-

MATERIALS LIST

Quantity	Size	Description	Location or Use
2	2¾ inches	1x4 #2 common pine	partitions
2	3½ inches	1x4 #2 common pine	ends
2	12 inches	1x4 #2 common pine	sides
1	10½ inches	1x4 #2 common pine	bottom
1 box	2-inch	galvanized finish nails	
1 bottle	8 oz.	carpenter's glue	
1 sheet	9x11 inches	40-grit sandpaper	
1 sheet	9x11 inches	60-grit sandpaper	
1 sheet	9x11 inches	120-grit sandpaper	
1 sheet	9x11 inches	220-grit sandpaper	
1 can	10 oz.	water-based wood putty	

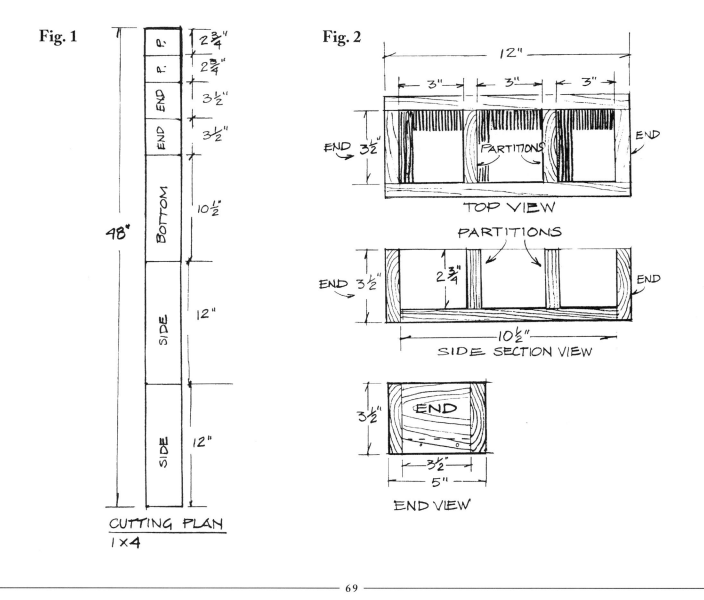

Fig. 1

CUTTING PLAN
1x4

Fig. 2

TOP VIEW

SIDE SECTION VIEW

END VIEW

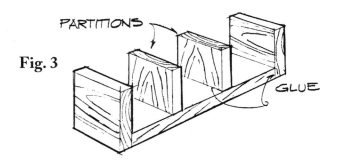

Fig. 3

PARTITIONS

GLUE

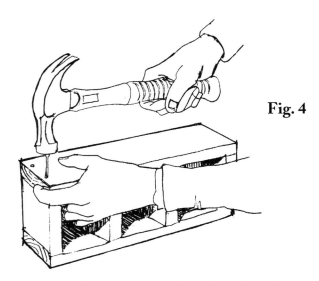

Fig. 4

fully measure and mark the wood where the first cut will be made. Using a combination square and a pencil (see p. 22, Fig. 15), draw a dark, heavy cut line across the wood. Then draw a lighter line on the "waste" side of the cut line. Position the saw between these two lines for a precise cut (see p. 27, Fig. 29).

With an electric jigsaw and speed square or with a handsaw and saw guide, cut the first piece 2¾ inches long. Referring to the Cutting Plan (see Fig. 1), measure, mark and cut each piece in succession, starting with the shortest pieces.

After cutting all the pieces but before nailing any of them together, place them in position, making sure they fit together perfectly. If there are any irregular edges that need to be trimmed, use a file or coarse (40-grit) sandpaper with a sanding block to straighten them (see p. 53-54 and Figs. 78 and 79).

Assembly is easier if you glue the pieces before nailing them together. Lay a bead of glue on the two outside edges of the bottom piece where the two end pieces will join the bottom. Place the two end pieces flush against the bottom piece and wait 10 minutes for the glue to begin setting. With a damp sponge, wipe off any glue that seeps out onto the wood. Next, glue the two partitions in place, spaced equally apart, to create three 3-inch-wide compartments (see Figs. 2 and 3).

Glue the side pieces last, overlapping the end pieces. After the glue has almost dried, hammer

two 2-inch finish nails ⅜ inch in from the edges of the box (see Fig. 4).

Be careful not to make dents in the wood when you are hammering in the nails. Hit the nail squarely and evenly on the head, and concentrate on keeping the hammer handle almost parallel to the wood (see p. 45, Figs. 58 and 59). Use a nail set to sink the nails just slightly below the surface of the wood (see Fig. 5 and p. 55, Fig. 85).

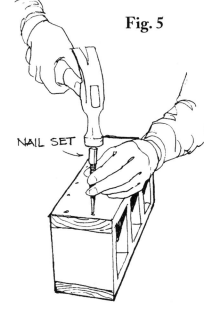

Fig. 5

NAIL SET

Fill all the nail holes with water-based wood putty, and sand the entire box when the putty has dried. Begin sanding with 60-grit sandpaper and a sanding block, smoothing any joints that may be slightly misaligned. Finish with 120-grit sandpaper, followed by 220-grit sandpaper, wrapped around a sanding block.

Carpenter's
TOOLBOX

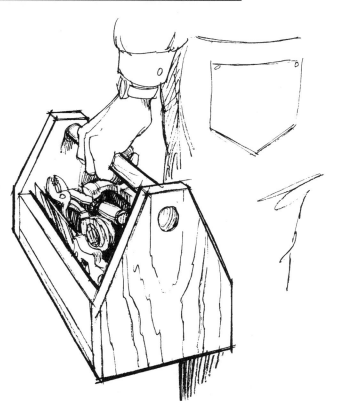

WHETHER YOU LIVE in an apartment or a house, chances are there will be times when you need a hammer, screwdriver or saw to make emergency repairs. When Jeanie was growing up, these basic tools were kept in the "mouse drawer," a catchall in which everything that did not have a place to go was found (including an occasional mouse!). A better idea is to have a toolbox that contains all of the essentials.

A list of the tools needed to build the projects in this book is included on p. 20. For home repairs, we suggest that you also invest in needle-nose and regular pliers, large vise-grip (locking) pliers, electrician's tape, a spackling knife and a utility knife.

Don't be tempted to buy a shiny, new metal toolbox instead of building this one. Metal boxes not only rust quickly, but they can also dull your tools—and they are noisy!

Our toolbox contains a compartment for loose hardware, has room for our Nail Box (see p. 68) and can even accommodate an 18-inch handsaw. If your handsaw happens to be longer, simply adjust the dimensions given here to the appropriate length. Another feature of our toolbox is that it uses standard-size lumber, which means it requires very little cutting. This is an easy project, and a good one to begin with.

Referring to the Cutting Plan (see Fig. 1), begin by cutting the end pieces and then the bottom. Clamp a 4-foot-long piece of 1x10 #2 pine

to a sturdy work surface. Make the two angled cuts for the end pieces by measuring and marking 6¼ inches down from both top corners of the board and then measuring and marking 3⅝ inches in from the top corners (see Fig. 2). Using a straightedge as your guide, draw a pencil line connecting these two points, and saw off the two angled corners with an electric jigsaw or a handsaw (see Fig. 3). From the end of the board, measure down 10½ inches and make a mark. Place a combination square (see p. 22, Fig. 15) flush against the side of the 1x10 and use it to draw a straight line across the board at the 10½-inch mark. Saw off this end piece. Turn the board around, clamp it to your work surface and follow the same steps to create the second end piece, so that you end up with two identical end pieces.

MATERIALS LIST

Quantity	Size	Description	Location or Use
2	18½ inches	1x4 #2 common pine	sides
2	10½ inches	1x10 #2 common pine	ends
1	18½ inches	1x10 #2 common pine	bottom
1	20 inches	1-inch-dia. dowel	handle
1 box	2-inch	galvanized finish nails	
1 can	10 oz.	water-based wood putty	
1 sheet	9x11 inches	60-grit sandpaper	
1 sheet	9x11 inches	120-grit sandpaper	
1 can	quart	wood sealer (optional)	

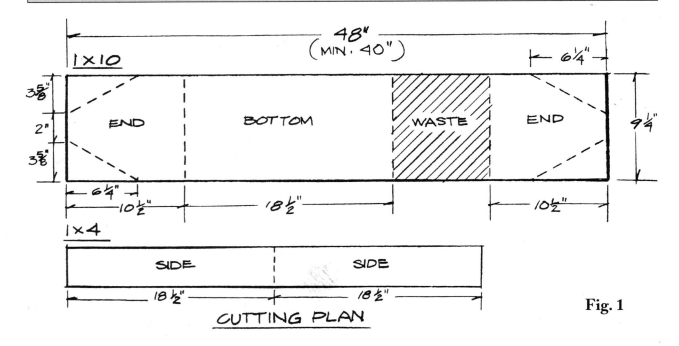

Fig. 1

Next, make the bottom of the toolbox. Clamp the remaining piece of 1x10 to the work surface. Measure and mark 18½ inches down from the end of the board. With a combination square flush against the side, draw a straight line across the board at the 18½-inch mark. Saw off the bottom piece.

To make the two identical side pieces, clamp the 1x4 to the work surface. Measure, mark and cut two pieces, each 18½ inches long. Check to make sure that the two sides and bottom piece are exactly the same length. Sand all five pieces until they are smooth, using 60-grit sandpaper, followed by 120-grit sandpaper, wrapped around a sanding block (see p. 53-54 and Figs. 78 and 79).

Using a combination square, find the center of each of the two end pieces and make a mark 1¼ inches down from the top of each. At this mark, use a 1-inch spade bit to drill out a 1-inch-diameter hole where the dowel handle will be positioned in each end piece (see Fig. 4 and p. 32, Fig. 41).

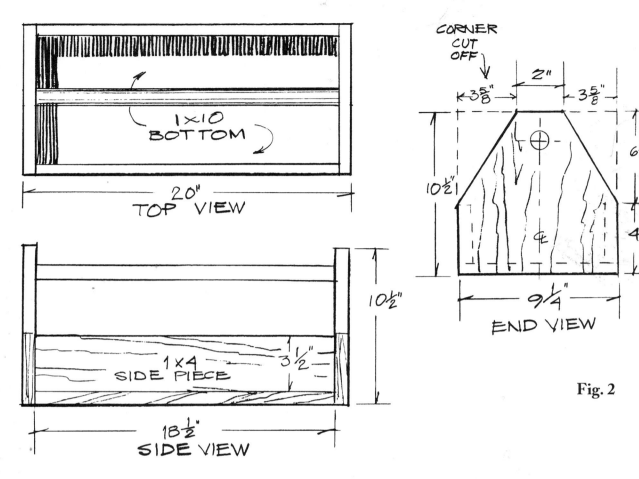

TOP VIEW

1×10 BOTTOM

20"

SIDE VIEW

1×4 SIDE PIECE

3 1/2"

10 1/2"

18 1/2"

END VIEW

CORNER CUT OFF

2"

3 5/8"   3 5/8"

10 1/2"

6 1/4"

4 1/4"

9 1/4"

Fig. 2

For the toolbox handle, use a handsaw to cut a 1-inch-diameter dowel so that it measures 20 inches long. To keep the dowel from rolling while you saw, use two clamps to secure it to your work surface. Twist one end of the dowel through the hole in an end piece, then do the same with the other end of the dowel and the remaining end piece (see Fig. 4). **NOTE:** Inserting the dowel at this stage makes the ends more stable, making it easier to install the bottom piece. Once the toolbox is assembled, it is much more difficult to get the dowel through the holes in the end pieces.

Next, turn the unit over on one end and wedge the bottom piece between the two end pieces. Nail the end piece to the bottom, hammering in 2-inch finish nails placed 3/8 inch from the edges and approximately 2 inches apart. Turn the unit over and repeat the process for the other end (see Fig. 5).

To attach the side pieces to the bottom and end pieces, keep the toolbox on end and wedge the side pieces between the two end pieces and on top of the bottom piece. Nail the end pieces to the side pieces, placing the nails 3/8 inch from the edge and approximately 1 inch apart. Turn the toolbox over on its side and, bracing it with one hand, nail the bottom piece to the bottom edge of the two side pieces, spacing the 2-inch finish nails approximately 2 inches apart (see Fig. 6). Turn the box over on the opposite side, and repeat the process.

To keep the handle in place, nail one 2-inch finish nail through the two slanted edges of each of the end pieces and into the 1-inch-diameter dowel (see Fig. 7).

Use a nail set to sink the finish nails just below the surface of the wood (see p. 55, Fig. 85).

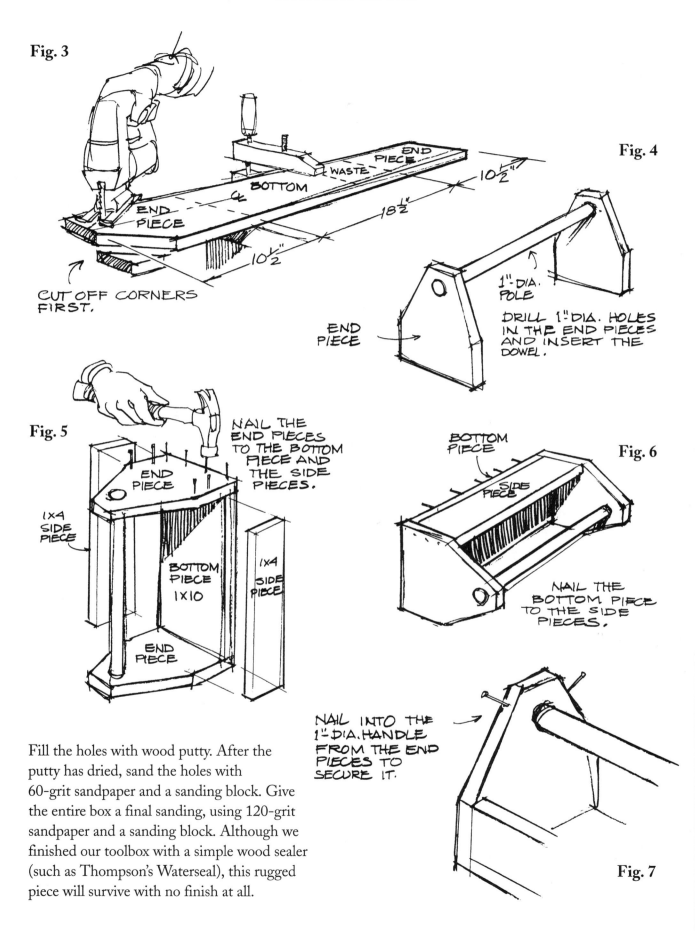

Fig. 3

CUT OFF CORNERS FIRST.

END PIECE

BOTTOM

WASTE

END PIECE

$10\frac{1}{2}''$

$18\frac{1}{2}''$

$10\frac{1}{2}''$

Fig. 4

END PIECE

1" DIA. POLE

DRILL 1" DIA. HOLES IN THE END PIECES AND INSERT THE DOWEL.

Fig. 5

NAIL THE END PIECES TO THE BOTTOM PIECE AND THE SIDE PIECES.

END PIECE

1X4 SIDE PIECE

BOTTOM PIECE 1X10

1X4 SIDE PIECE

END PIECE

BOTTOM PIECE

SIDE PIECE

Fig. 6

NAIL THE BOTTOM PIECE TO THE SIDE PIECES.

NAIL INTO THE 1" DIA. HANDLE FROM THE END PIECES TO SECURE IT.

Fig. 7

Fill the holes with wood putty. After the putty has dried, sand the holes with 60-grit sandpaper and a sanding block. Give the entire box a final sanding, using 120-grit sandpaper and a sanding block. Although we finished our toolbox with a simple wood sealer (such as Thompson's Waterseal), this rugged piece will survive with no finish at all.

Letter
B O X

THIS SIMPLE BOX, with its pleasing shape and practical size, can store not only letters but bills, envelopes, stamps—almost anything that accumulates on your desk or dresser. We based the measurements of our letter box on a typical #10 envelope, which is 9½ inches long by 4 inches high. We designed the width of our box to be 3½ inches. This latter dimension can vary, depending on what and how much you want your box to hold. For a box this small, we recommend using ½x4 lumber (actually ⁷⁄₁₆ inch thick); ¾-inch-thick lumber would make it look out of scale.

All five pieces of the letter box can be cut from one 48-inch-long ½x4 clear pine board.

Before you do any measuring or cutting, check first to make sure the lumber has square ends. If not, mark each end with a speed square or combination square (see p. 21-23 and Figs. 15 and 23) and cut them off squarely. You can use an electric jigsaw and a speed square (see p. 27, Fig. 30) for the cuts, but it's easier to make accurate cuts with a handsaw and saw guide (see p. 63).

If you are using a saw guide, slide the board under the triangle, making sure that the board is held tightly against the fence of the guide. Since you are using ⁷⁄₁₆-inch-thick lumber and the space inside the guide is ¾ inch, you'll need to clamp the board securely to the guide before making your cuts.

MATERIALS LIST

Quantity	Size	Description	Location or Use
2	3½ inches	½x4 clear pine	ends
2	10¾ inches	½x4 clear pine	front & back
1	9⅞ inches	½x4 clear pine	bottom
1 box	1½-inch	finish nails	
1 box	1-inch	galvanized wire nails	
1 bottle	8 oz.	carpenter's glue	
1 sheet	9x11 inches	40-grit sandpaper	
1 sheet	9x11 inches	60-grit sandpaper	
1 sheet	9x11 inches	80-grit sandpaper	
1 sheet	9x11 inches	120-grit sandpaper	
1 sheet	9x11 inches	220-grit sandpaper	
1 can	10 oz.	water-based wood putty	
1 can	quart	paint, stain or wood sealer	
1 can		wax	

Referring to the Cutting Plan (see Fig. 1), measure, mark and cut each piece separately, always cutting on the "waste" side of the board to ensure an accurate cut. To make this step easier, draw two lines on the board—the first, and darker, one at the measured mark; the second, and fainter, one on the waste side of the board, ¹⁄₁₆ to ⅛ inch from the first line (the width of the saw blade). Make your cut in the space between these two lines (see p. 27, Fig. 29).

Cut the two end pieces first, followed by the front, back and bottom, sliding the piece of lumber through the guide after each cut. Remember to clean the sawdust out of the saw guide between cuts.

Fig. 1

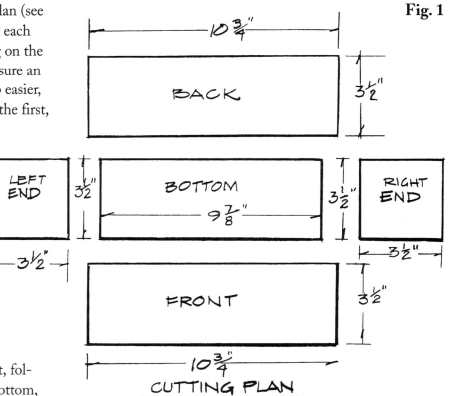

CUTTING PLAN

Fig. 2

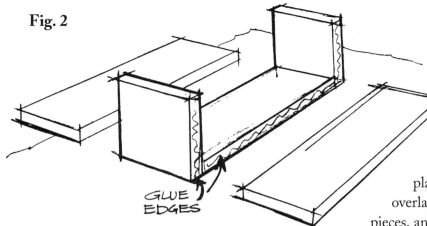

GLUE
EDGES

After cutting out the five pieces, lay them in place (see Fig. 1) and label each one lightly in pencil where it won't show after the box is assembled. Sand any uneven edges until they are perfectly square, using 40-grit sandpaper and a sanding block (see p. 53-54 and Figs. 78 and 79). Do not round off the edges while you are sanding, as they should fit together squarely when you assemble the box.

Before putting the box together, sand all the surfaces that will face *inside* the box, as this is impossible to do effectively once the box is assembled. An electric palm sander (see p. 55, Fig. 81) with 80-grit sandpaper is a useful tool for smoothing the inside surfaces. Or use 120-grit sandpaper and a sanding block.

Now, remind yourself which pieces of the box will have overlapping edges. Place the bottom piece on a sheet of waxed paper, squeeze a thin bead of glue around its outside edges (see Fig. 2) and spread the glue evenly with a flat stick. Use a damp sponge to wipe off any glue that might have smeared onto the surface of the wood; otherwise, the glue will stain the wood.

Next, squeeze a thin bead of glue along the side edges of the two end pieces and spread it evenly with a flat stick. Again, wipe off any excess glue. Position the end pieces so they are flush against the end edges of the bottom piece (see Fig. 2). Then place the front and back pieces so they overlap the edges of the bottom and end pieces, and align them so all edges are flush with one another.

After the glue has dried for 10 minutes, hammer two 1-inch galvanized wire nails ¼ inch in from the edge of each front and back piece (see Fig. 3), spacing the nails equally. Then hammer three 1½-inch finish nails, evenly spaced, along the bottom of the front and the back pieces. **NOTE:** Do not allow the glue to dry for more than 10 minutes, as it will restrict the pieces from being nailed securely.

After the box is firmly glued and nailed together, inspect it for any misaligned joints or edges and sand them off, using 40-grit sandpaper

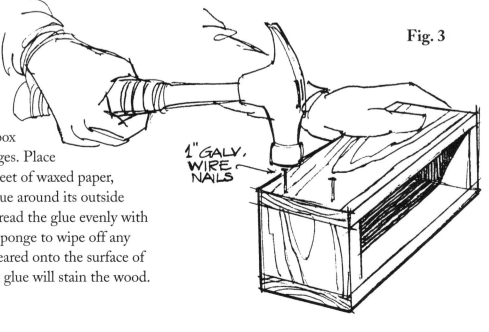

Fig. 3

1" GALV.
WIRE
NAILS

Fig. 4

and a sanding block or an electric palm or orbital sander.

If desired, cut a shallow curve out of the front piece of the letter box for easier access to its contents. Using a quart-sized paint can as a guide, trace a curve onto the wood and cut it out with an electric jigsaw (see Fig. 4 and p. 28, Fig. 32). Sand the curve with 60-grit sandpaper wrapped around a cylindrical object, such as a bottle or can, followed by 120-grit sandpaper (see p. 100, Fig. 4).

Use a nail set (see p. 55, Fig. 85) to sink the nail heads slightly below the surface of the wood, and fill the holes with wood putty. When the putty has dried, sand the entire box again, using 220-grit sandpaper and a sanding block. As you sand, watch how the grain and the color of the wood begin to stand out as the surface becomes smoother. It will not only look good but also feel good—almost like satin.

There are a variety of ways to finish the box—with paint, stain or clear wood sealer followed by a couple of applications of hand-rubbed wax. The clearest wax we have found, which doesn't turn yellow, is Briwax (see p. 56). It is more expensive than many other waxes but gives a beautiful, soft finish.

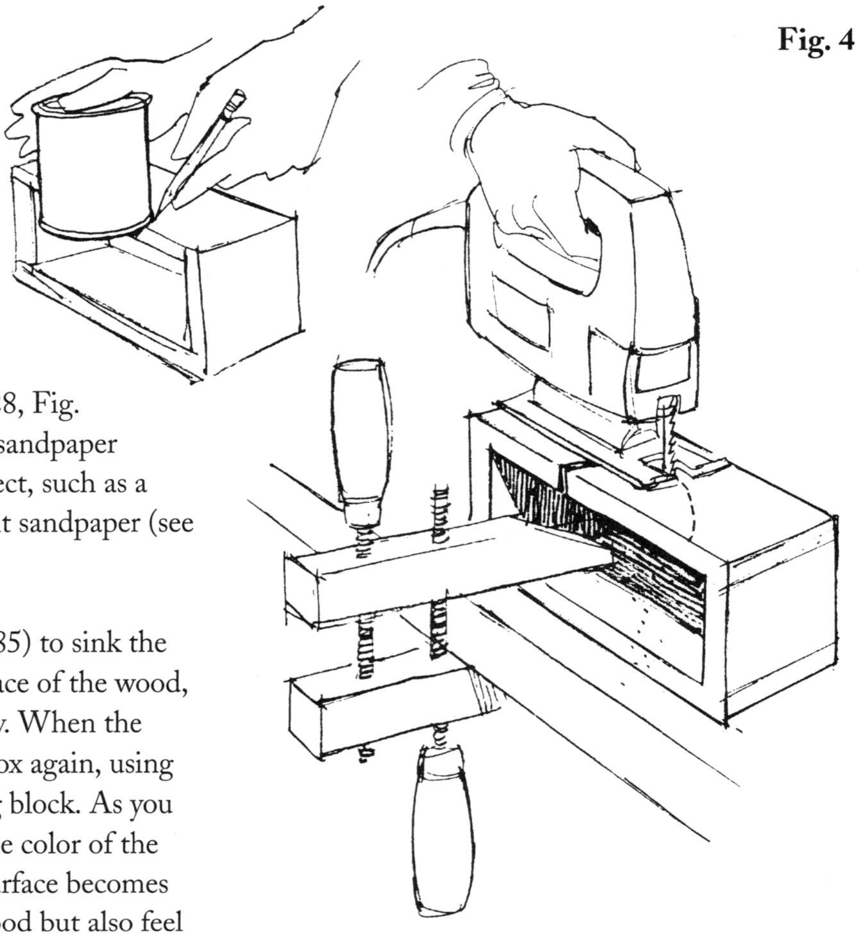

Under-Bed
STORAGE BOX

E VERYONE CAN USE more storage space, and a perfect spot is the unused space under a bed. This Under-Bed Storage Box is ideal for out-of-season clothes or exercise attire, extra blankets, sheets and pillowcases, even a wedding dress. The box illustrated here, made using 1x6 lumber for the sides, fits perfectly under our platform bed. If you have more than 6 inches of vertical space under your bed, you may want to increase the height of the front and back panels of the box from 5¾ inches to 7½ inches and change the 1x6 in the Materials List to a 1x8.

If you don't mind paying a nominal milling fee, you might want to ask your lumberyard to cut the plywood pieces for you, according to the Cut-

ting Plan (see Fig. 1). If you prefer to do it yourself, use a measuring tape and framing square (see p. 23, Fig. 21) to mark the cut lines on the plywood (good side up), following the layout and measurements given. **NOTE:** The Cutting Plan shows how to cut three boxes from one full sheet of plywood. If you want to build only one box, buy half a sheet of plywood and adjust the Cutting Plan accordingly.

After double-checking your measurements for accuracy, place the plywood (good side up) on a sturdy work surface and cut out the top, bottom, back and front pieces, using a fine-toothed cross-cut handsaw (see Fig. 2). Hold the saw as parallel to the wood as possible to minimize splintering,

MATERIALS LIST (FOR ONE BOX)

Quantity	Size	Description	Location or Use
1	24½x18 inches	¼-inch exterior plywood	sliding top panel
1	24x18 inches	¼-inch exterior plywood	bottom
2	5¾x18 inches	¼-inch exterior plywood	front & back
2	24 inches	1x6 #2 common pine	sides
1	18½ inches	¼x1½-inch lattice	front trim
2	24 inches	¼x1½-inch lattice	side trim
1 box	1-inch	galvanized wire nails	
1 bottle	8 oz.	carpenter's glue	
1 sheet	9x11 inches	60-grit sandpaper	
1 sheet	9x11 inches	120-grit sandpaper	
1 sheet	9x11 inches	220-grit sandpaper	

Fig. 1

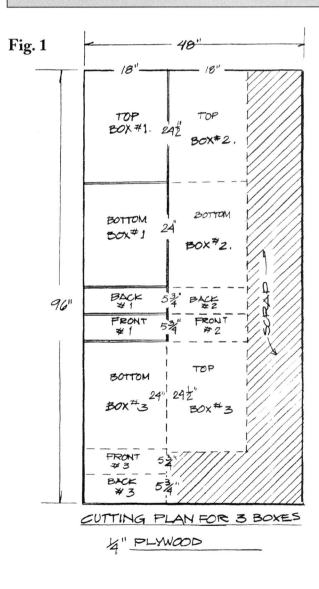

CUTTING PLAN FOR 3 BOXES

¼" PLYWOOD

Fig. 2

or tear-out (see p. 31), on the underneath side of the plywood. Using 60-grit sandpaper and a sanding block (see p. 53-54 and Figs. 78 and 79), sand the edges of the plywood until they are straight and smooth (see Fig. 3). Then use 120-grit sandpaper to sand all the surfaces that will be facing inside the box, as it will be difficult to sand them after the box is assembled.

Fig. 3

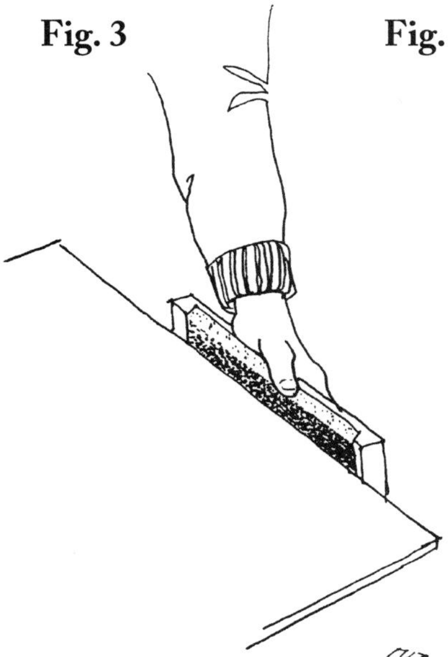

Fig. 4

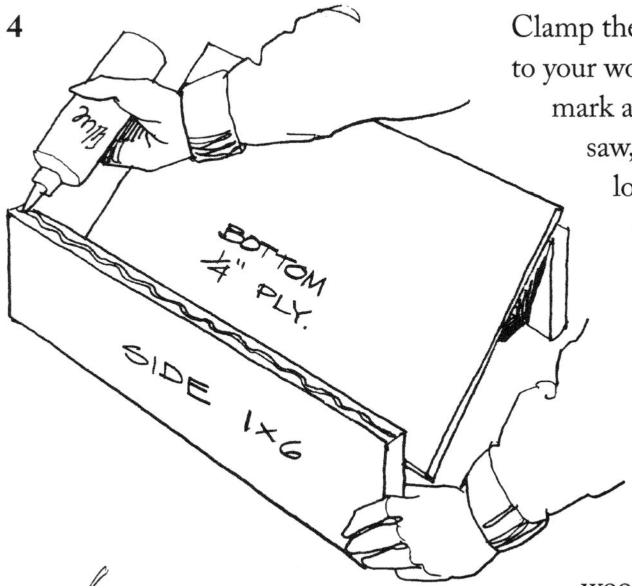

Fig. 5

Fig. 6

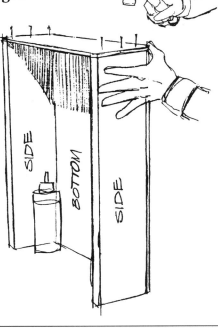

Clamp the 1x6 #2 pine board to your work surface. Measure, mark and cut, using a handsaw, each of the 24-inch-long side pieces. Stand one of the two side pieces up on its long edge and squeeze a thin bead of glue along the top edge (see Fig. 4). Repeat for the second side piece. Carefully lay the plywood bottom on top of the two glue-covered side edges, covering one edge at a time. Check to see that the edges are perfectly aligned, then start a 1-inch galvanized wire nail in each of the four corners of the bottom piece. Check again for proper alignment before driving the nails in all the way. Hammer four more nails along each bottom edge and into the sides (see Fig. 5).

Turn the partially assembled unit on end. Squeeze a bead of glue on the ends of the two side pieces and the bottom piece. Carefully place the front piece over the glue-covered edges and hammer three 1-inch galvanized wire nails, equally spaced, through the front piece and into the ends of the side pieces (see Fig. 6). Turn the unit over and follow the same procedure for the other side, gluing and nailing the back piece to the sides.

Holding the front end up, carefully nail three 1-inch galvanized wire nails, equally spaced, through the front piece and into the glued edges of the bottom. Take time to do this right, as there is not much room for error when nailing into ¼-inch-thick plywood (see Fig. 7). Repeat the procedure, nailing the back piece to the bottom of the box. These nails will hold the front

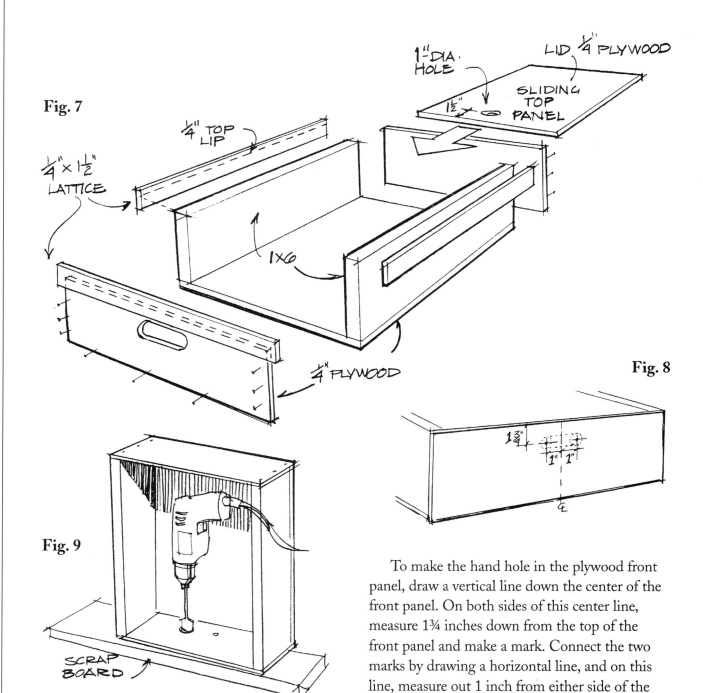

Fig. 7

¼" TOP LIP

¼" × 1½" LATTICE

1×6

¼" PLYWOOD

1" DIA. HOLE

LID ¼" PLYWOOD

1½" × ○

SLIDING TOP PANEL

Fig. 8

1¾"

1" 1"

℄

Fig. 9

SCRAP BOARD

and back pieces to the bottom piece while the glue is drying.

After the glue has dried, use 120-grit sandpaper and a sanding block to sand all the edges and outside surfaces of the pieces. **NOTE:** Be careful not to lay the box down on anything sharp, as the surface of the wood can be easily dented.

To make the hand hole in the plywood front panel, draw a vertical line down the center of the front panel. On both sides of this center line, measure 1¾ inches down from the top of the front panel and make a mark. Connect the two marks by drawing a horizontal line, and on this line, measure out 1 inch from either side of the center line and make a cross mark (see Fig. 8).

Turn the box on end, front side up. Using a 1-inch spade bit in a VSR electric drill, partially drill two holes at the cross marks, going just far enough to cut through the first ply of the plywood. Turn the box over so that the front side is down, and place it on top of a piece of scrap wood. With the box in this position, finish drilling out the holes from the inside of the box

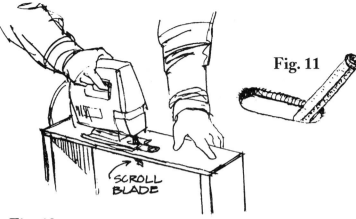

Fig. 11

Fig. 10

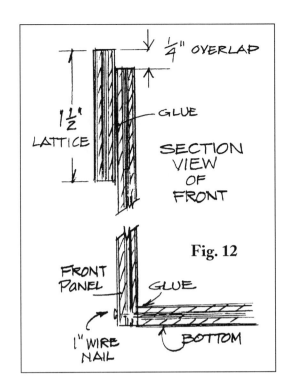

Fig. 12

(see Fig. 9). This method avoids splitting the plywood when the drill exits the hole.

Turn the box over again so the front side is up. With a framing square, draw two parallel lines connecting the two holes and creating the elongated shape shown in Fig. 11. Using an electric jigsaw, cut along these lines to remove the material between the two holes (see Fig. 10). **NOTE:** Use a fine-toothed (scroll) blade to prevent splintering the edge.

Use the same technique to make a 1-inch-diameter hole in the sliding top panel, centered 1½ inches in from the front edge of the panel (see Fig. 7). Round off and smooth both holes with a rolled up piece of 120-grit sandpaper (see Fig. 11).

Use an electric jigsaw with a fine-toothed (scroll) blade to cut the three pieces of ¼x1½-inch lattice: one measuring 18½ inches long and two measuring 24 inches long. Glue and clamp the 18½-inch-long piece of lattice to the top of the front panel so that the top edge of the lattice

overlaps the top edge and each of the side edges of the front panel by ¼ inch (see Fig. 12).

Clamp and glue a 24-inch-long piece of lattice trim to one side of the box so that it overlaps the top edge of the side by ¼ inch. Repeat this procedure on the other side of the box with the remaining 24-inch-long piece. The three pieces of lattice form a ¼-inch lip on three sides of the box, with the ends of the front panel overlapping the ends of the side pieces.

Position the sliding top panel between the two side lips so that it slides easily along the top edges of the two 1x6 sides of the box (see Fig. 7).

Sand the outside surfaces of the box with 220-grit sandpaper and a sanding block, and apply a finish of your choice.

Toy

CHEST

A TOY CHEST is a practical piece of furniture for any child's room. It not only provides a good place to store toys, stuffed animals and board games, but it also makes a nice bench for kids to sit on. Our toy chest, built from birch plywood, is fairly lightweight and can be decorated in any number of ways. Use your imagination: Dinosaurs, sailboats, bunny rabbits, flowers or your child's initials could be stenciled onto it. Or use a jigsaw to cut wood into different figures, shapes or designs and glue them to the front.

After your kids outgrow the chest, it can still come in handy. Use it as a blanket chest, stock it with sheets and towels in a guest room or store woolen clothes in it, along with some cedar shavings.

All the pieces of the toy chest can be cut from one 4x8-foot sheet of ¾-inch-thick birch plywood. Following the measurements shown on the Cutting Plan (see Fig. 1), use a T-square and pencil, or a chalk line, to mark the cut lines on the side of the plywood that won't be visible when it's assembled.

The plywood can be cut with a handsaw, but the cuts will be more difficult and less accurate. If you are using a handsaw, first run a utility knife over the cut lines, cutting through the first ply only on the underneath side of the plywood to avoid tear-out (see p. 31). Then cut out the pieces with your handsaw.

We recommend, instead, using a circular saw fitted with a sharp, fine-toothed blade made expressly for cutting plywood. Clamp a straight-

MATERIALS LIST

Quantity	Size	Description	Location or Use
2	13½x35 inches	¾-inch birch plywood	front & back
2	13½x16½ inches	¾-inch birch plywood	sides
1	18½x36 inches	¾-inch birch plywood	top
1	16½x34 inches	¾-inch birch plywood	bottom
1 box	2-inch	finish nails	
1 bottle	8 oz.	carpenter's glue	
1 sheet	9x11 inches	40-grit sandpaper	
1 sheet	9x11 inches	60-grit sandpaper	
1 sheet	9x11 inches	120-grit sandpaper	
1 sheet	9x11 inches	220-grit sandpaper	
1 can	10 oz.	water-based wood putty	
1	35 inches	1-inch continuous (piano) hinge with screws	lid hinge
1 pair		spring-loaded side lid supports	
2	12 inches	⅝-inch-dia. rope	handles
1 can	quart	clear wood finish or paint	
1 set of 4		nylon swivel glides	

edged 1x6 to the plywood to act as a guide for the saw (see p. 28, Fig. 34). **NOTE:** Be careful when you are handling and sawing the plywood that you do not mar the surface of the wood. This can save you hours of sanding later on.

After cutting out the pieces, the edges may be a little rough and irregular and need to be sanded. Instead of the usual sanding block (sandpaper wrapped around a piece of wood), take 5 minutes to make an edge-sanding block designed expressly for this purpose. With a handsaw, cut two pieces of 1x4, each 12 inches long. Take a scrap piece of ¾-inch plywood (the same thickness as the plywood you are sanding) and cut it to 1½x12 inches (see Fig. 2). With a framing square as a guide (see p. 54, Fig. 78), tear a 9-inch-long piece of 40-grit sandpaper 3 inches wide and fold it around the ¾-inch plywood scrap. Screw the two pieces of 1x4 to either side of the sandpaper-cov-

ered plywood, sandwiching it between them (see Fig. 2). This edge-sanding block is much easier to use and prevents accidentally sanding at an angle. Remember, in this situation, the purpose of sanding is not to make the edges smooth but to make them absolutely square and straight. To change the sandpaper, remove the screws from the 1x4s, reposition or replace the sandpaper, put the screws back in and continue.

To assemble the plywood pieces, place the bottom piece on a stable work surface and make sure one end is supported against something solid (see Fig. 3). Squeeze a bead of carpenter's glue on the side edge of the bottom piece. Position one of the side pieces so it overlaps and is flush with the edge of the bottom piece. Nail five 2-inch finish nails through the outside of the side piece and into the edge of the bottom piece (see Fig. 3). Turn the unit around, and repeat the same proce-

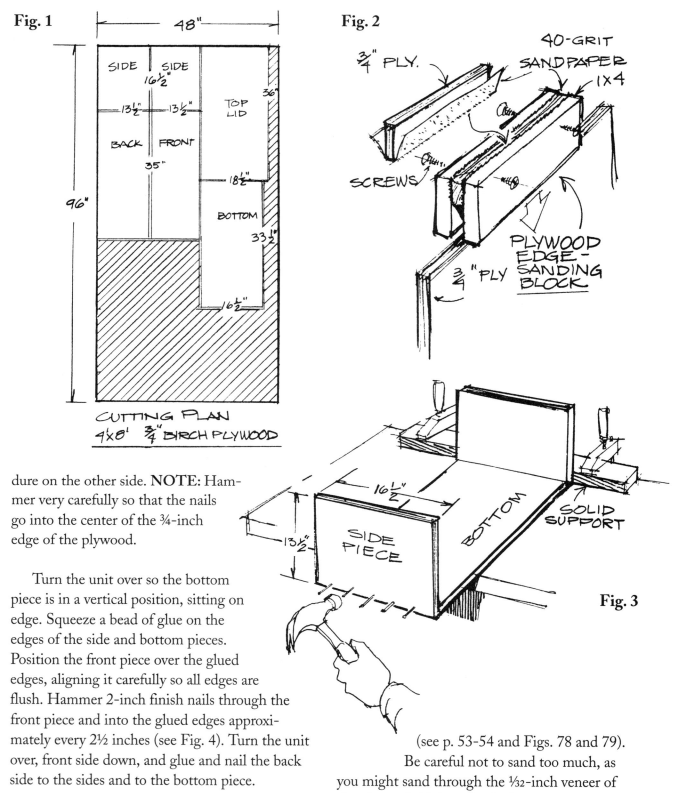

Fig. 1

48"

SIDE | SIDE
16½"

13½" — 13½"

TOP LID
36"

BACK | FRONT

35"

18½"

96"

BOTTOM

33½"

16½"

CUTTING PLAN
4'x8' ¾" BIRCH PLYWOOD

Fig. 2

¾" PLY.

40-GRIT SANDPAPER

1X4

SCREWS

¾" PLY

PLYWOOD EDGE-SANDING BLOCK

Fig. 3

16½"

13½"

SIDE PIECE

BOTTOM

SOLID SUPPORT

dure on the other side. **NOTE:** Hammer very carefully so that the nails go into the center of the ¾-inch edge of the plywood.

Turn the unit over so the bottom piece is in a vertical position, sitting on edge. Squeeze a bead of glue on the edges of the side and bottom pieces. Position the front piece over the glued edges, aligning it carefully so all edges are flush. Hammer 2-inch finish nails through the front piece and into the glued edges approximately every 2½ inches (see Fig. 4). Turn the unit over, front side down, and glue and nail the back side to the sides and to the bottom piece.

When the glue has dried, sand the edges, corners and surfaces of the plywood with 60-, 120- and 220-grit sandpaper and a sanding block

(see p. 53-54 and Figs. 78 and 79).
Be careful not to sand too much, as you might sand through the $\frac{1}{32}$-inch veneer of the plywood. To be safe, don't use a power sander to do this job; do it by hand only. Use a nail set (see p. 55, Fig. 85) to sink all the nail heads below the surface of the plywood, and fill the nail holes

with wood putty. After the wood putty has dried, sand the surfaces smooth with 220-grit sandpaper.

With a hack-saw, cut 1 inch off the piano hinge, making it 35 inches long. Using a small Phillips screwdriver, screw the piano hinge to the rear top edge of the chest and then to the underside of the top lid (see Fig. 5, Hinge Detail).

To keep the lid from slamming down on little fingers, attach two spring-loaded, self-balancing side lid supports according to the directions that accompany them.

We attached rope handles to the sides of our toy chest to make it easier to move. To do this, draw a vertical line down the center of one side. Next, 2½ inches on either side of this center line, make a mark 4 inches down from the top of the side (see Fig. 5, Side Section). Use a ¾-inch spade bit (see p. 31, Fig. 40) to make a hole at both marks. Tie a knot in one end of one of the ropes and, starting inside the box, thread it through one hole and back through the other. Then, leaving enough slack on the outside of the chest to create a handle, tie a knot in its end. Repeat this procedure for the other side.

Finish the toy chest by sanding it smooth with 220-grit sandpaper and a sanding block.

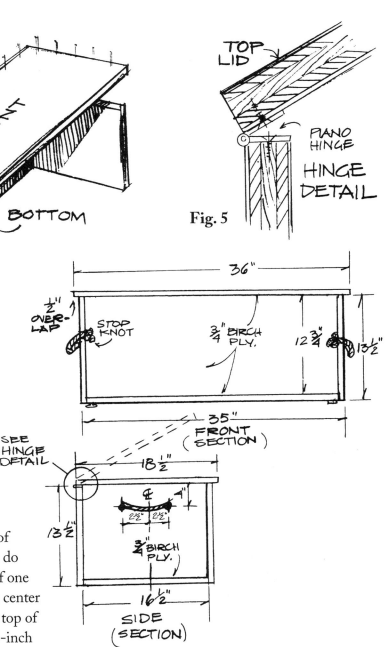

Brush on two or three coats of clear wood finish (we recommend Varathane's clear satin Elite Diamond Finish) or paint the plywood with two coats of semi-gloss or gloss paint, which is easier to keep clean.

To protect your floor, attach the nylon swivel glides by nailing them to the bottom four corners of the chest.

A-Frame
MAILBOX

A MAILBOX IS OFTEN the first impression someone has of your house. By making your own, you can add a personal and distinctive touch—even perk up the mail carrier's route. Before installing it, be sure to check with the post office regarding the specifications for height and placement of the mailbox.

This easy-to-build project can be constructed in only half a day. Since the front and back pieces are small and get a lot of exposure, we splurged and bought 2 feet of 1x10 clear mahogany; however, you can use cedar, teak or any other wood that is durable and weather-resistant.

Begin by cutting the triangular front and back pieces as shown in the Cutting Plan (see Fig. 1). Clamp the 2-foot piece of 1x10 to your work table. With a tape measure and pencil, measure and mark 11½ inches down from the end. Draw a line across the board at this point and cut the piece off with a handsaw or electric jigsaw (see p. 27, Fig. 30). Repeat this procedure on the remaining piece of 1x10.

Clamp one of the 1x10s to your work surface and draw a vertical line down the center. From the top of the center line, draw a line down to one bottom corner. Draw another line from the top of the center line and down to the other corner. Cut out this triangular piece with a handsaw or an electric jigsaw. Repeat these steps with the remaining 1x10. **NOTE:** Do not cut off the top 3 inches of the front triangle yet.

Use 60-grit sandpaper and a sanding block (see p. 53-54 and Figs. 78 and 79) to make the edges of both triangles straight, then smooth them using 120-grit sandpaper.

To make the floor piece, cut the 2x10 to measure 14½ inches long and use an electric jigsaw

MATERIALS LIST

Quantity	Size	Description	Location or Use
1	6 feet	4x4 pressure-treated post	post
2	11½ inches	1x10 cedar, teak or mahogany	front & back
1	14½ inches	2x10 fir	floor
1	14 inches	2x4 cedar	floor support
2	14 inches	2x6 cedar	brackets
1	14½ inches	2x2 cedar	ridgepole
12	18 inches	red cedar shingles	roof
1	4x20 inches	copper flashing	roof trim
1	8 inches	1-inch continuous (piano) hinge with screws	door hinge
1		roller friction catch with screws	door catch
1 box	1½-inch	galvanized finish nails	shingles
1 box	2-inch	galvanized finish nails	back & floor
1 box	⅝-inch	bronze or copper nails	roof
1 box	2¼-inch	#10 galvanized deck screws	
1 sheet	9x11 inches	60-grit sandpaper	
1 sheet	9x11 inches	120-grit sandpaper	
1 sheet	9x11 inches	220-grit sandpaper	

(or block plane) to bevel both edges 22 degrees toward the center (see Fig. 2). To establish this angle, either use a protractor or measure over ⅝ inch from each top side edge and start your bevel at this point.

To make the ridgepole, cut the 2x2 to measure 14½ inches long. Trim off the top corner edges at a 22-degree angle, using an electric jigsaw or block plane (see Fig. 3). With a twist bit in an electric drill (see p. 31, Fig. 40), make a ⅛-inch pilot hole 2¼ inches down from the top of both triangles (see Fig. 1). Position the bottom of the ridgepole so that it is 3 inches below the top of the triangle, and screw a 2¼-inch #10 galvanized deck screw through each of the triangles and into the ends of the ridgepole. One screw is permanent; the other, temporary (see Fig. 4).

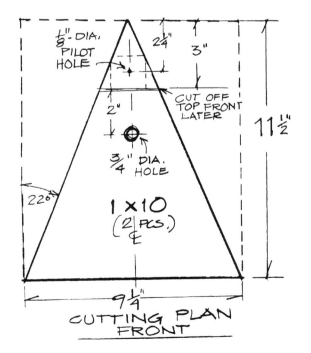

Fig. 1

Fig. 2

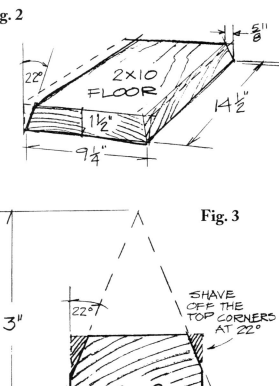

Fig. 3

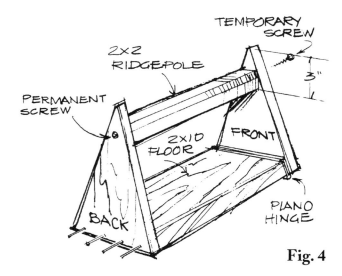

Fig. 4

Use a hacksaw to cut the 1-inch piano hinge 8 inches long. (If you don't have a hacksaw, substitute two 1½x3-inch galvanized butt hinges for the piano hinge.) Screw the hinge onto the inside bottom face of the mailbox door and the front end of the 2x10 floor (see Fig. 4). Nail the triangular back piece to the floor using four 2-inch galvanized finish nails, equally spaced.

Cover one side of the mailbox with a layer of cedar shingles. Use any width shingles, just as long as their total combined width is 19 inches. Place the shingles on one side of the mailbox, so that they overlap the bottom and each of the two ends by 1½ inches, and nail them in place, hammering two 1½-inch galvanized finish nails in each shingle. **NOTE:** Be careful not to nail through the shingles into the front triangular

piece (which becomes the front door), or it will not be able to swing open (see Fig. 5). Nail only along the floor and ridgepole and along the back triangle.

After you have covered one side with a layer of shingles, lay the box flat on your work table, shingle side down. Hold your handsaw so that the blade is parallel with the edge of the triangle and the beveled ridgepole, and cut the shingles off at a 22-degree angle (see Fig. 6). Repeat the shingling process on the other side of the mailbox, until both sides of the roof are covered with two layers of shingles. Make sure the second layer of shingles is staggered so that the spaces between the shingles don't line up.

To prevent rain from leaking in through the top, bend a 4x20-inch piece of copper flashing over the peak and the two ends (see Fig. 7). Nail the copper to the ridge with ⅝-inch bronze (boat) nails or copper nails, spaced every 2½ inches.

Remove the front triangle by unscrewing the temporary screw at the top and the hinge underneath. To allow the front door to swing open, you must cut across the top of the front piece, separating the top triangular portion of the triangle, which will remain attached to the ridgepole. To

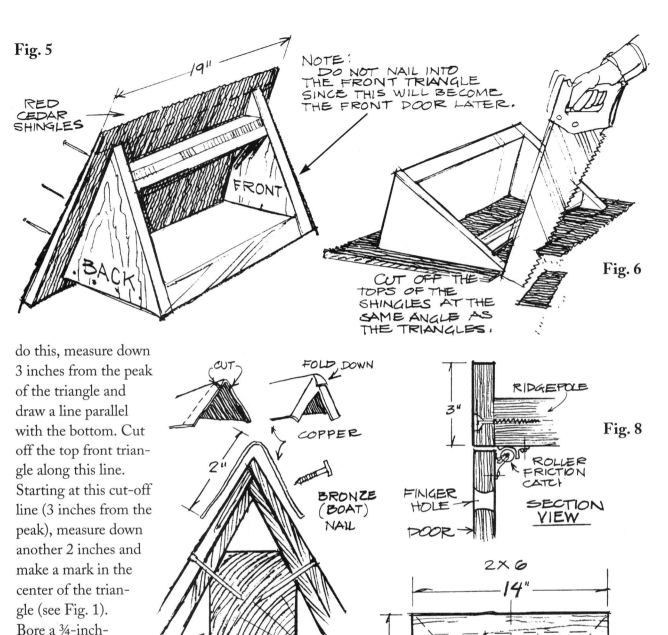

Fig. 5

19"

RED CEDAR SHINGLES

FRONT

BACK

NOTE: DO NOT NAIL INTO THE FRONT TRIANGLE SINCE THIS WILL BECOME THE FRONT DOOR LATER.

Fig. 6

CUT OFF THE TOPS OF THE SHINGLES AT THE SAME ANGLE AS THE TRIANGLES.

CUT

FOLD DOWN

COPPER

2"

BRONZE (BOAT) NAIL

RIDGEPOLE

Fig. 7

3"

RIDGEPOLE

FINGER HOLE

DOOR

ROLLER FRICTION CATCH

SECTION VIEW

Fig. 8

2 X 6

14"

5½"

¢

CUT OFF

CUT OFF

1¾" 1¾"

3½"

Fig. 9

do this, measure down 3 inches from the peak of the triangle and draw a line parallel with the bottom. Cut off the top front triangle along this line. Starting at this cut-off line (3 inches from the peak), measure down another 2 inches and make a mark in the center of the triangle (see Fig. 1). Bore a ¾-inch-diameter hole (see p. 32, Fig. 41) or screw on a knob of your choice. Replace the front door by reattaching the piano hinge. Use a dowel wrapped with sandpaper (see p. 54, Fig. 79) to sand the finger hole, starting with 60-grit and followed by 120- and 220-grit sandpaper.

To make sure that your door fits tightly and will stay closed, install a roller friction catch at the top of the door. This catch comes with its own screws and instructions and is easily attached to

the door and to the underneath part of the ridge-pole (see Fig. 8).

Next, build a wooden bracket on which to mount the mailbox. Cut two pieces of 2x6, each measuring 14 inches long, and one piece of 2x4

Fig. 10

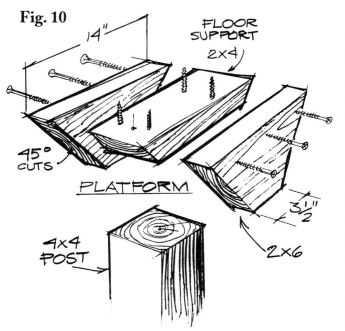

14" FLOOR SUPPORT 2x4

45° CUTS

PLATFORM

4x4 POST

3½"

2x6

measuring 14 inches long. Find the center (7 inches) of the 2x6s, and measure and mark 1¾ inch on either side to indicate where the 6-foot-long 4x4 post (actually 3½ inches square) will go (see Fig. 9). Draw a diagonal line from the top corners of the 2x6s to the points you have just made and saw off the lower corners (approximately 45 degrees) to form a "V" with a flattened 3½-inch-wide bottom.

To make the middle section of the bracket, make 45-degree angled cuts at both ends of the

Fig. 12

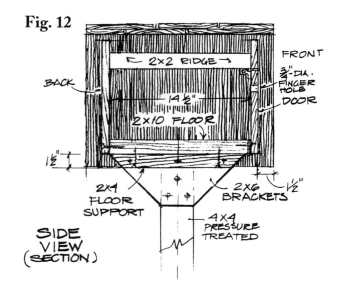

BACK
2x2 RIDGE
FRONT
3"-DIA. FINGER HOLE
DOOR
14½"
2x10 FLOOR
1½"
2x4 FLOOR SUPPORT
2x6 BRACKETS
1½"
4x4 PRESSURE TREATED
SIDE VIEW (SECTION)

14-inch-long 2x4. Line up the top edges of the two 2x6 brackets and the 2x4 floor support and screw the 2x6s to either side of the 2x4. Use six 2¼-inch galvanized deck screws, starting the screws ¾ inch down from the top edge of the brackets (see Fig. 10).

Dig a 2-foot-deep hole where the mailbox will be installed and place a flat stone or brick at the bottom. Place one end of the pressure-treated 4x4 in the hole and gradually backfill, tamping down the soil as you fill the hole. Use a level to check that it's plumb. We allowed 4 feet of the post to stick out of the ground, so our car's mirror would not hit the mailbox when we drive past to pick up our mail (see Fig. 11).

Using four 2¼-inch galvanized deck screws, secure the platform bracket onto the bottom of the mailbox floor. Screw through the 2x4 and into the underneath side of the mailbox floor. Attach the bracketed mailbox assembly to the post by slipping the mailbox bracket over the end of the post and securing it with three 2¼-inch screws on each side, equally spaced in a triangular pattern (see Fig. 12).

Fig. 11

16" 11½" PIANO HINGE 2x4 2x6 9¼" 4x4 4' 2' BRICK

Open
SHELVES

YOU MAY WANT TO DESIGN and build open shelves that fit your own specifications rather than use the dimensions included here. If so, it would be helpful to review the information about building shelves on p. 58-59. As you work on the design, remember to measure your tallest books or decorative items and make sure at least one set of shelves can accommodate them, allowing ½ inch for clearance (see Fig. 1).

We chose 1x10 #2 common pine for this project for two reasons: This size board fits most books and #2 pine is more economical than clear pine. Since the shelves are covered with books, we felt that spending extra money on clear pine was unnecessary. To strengthen the unit and give

it a more substantial, built-in look, we trimmed the edges with 1x2 #2 clear poplar.

Before beginning this project, measure your ceiling height to make sure that you will have at least 1 inch of clearance between the ceiling and the top of the bookcase for installation. If the 8-foot uprights are too long for your ceiling, cut them to the appropriate height. Stand them up again and mark a profile of where the baseboard of your wall meets the bottom back of both uprights (see Fig. 2).

Next, carefully measure and mark the two 1x10s that will be used for the shelves. Each shelf should be exactly the same length. Use either a

MATERIALS LIST

Quantity	Size	Description	Location or Use
2	8 feet	1x10 #2 common pine	uprights
6	40 inches	1x10 #2 common pine	shelves
2	8 feet	1x2 #2 clear poplar	upright trim
6	38½ inches	1x2 #2 clear poplar	shelf trim
1	40 inches	1x2 #2 clear poplar	support board
1 box	1½-inch	finish nails	
1 box	2-inch	finish nails	
1 box	3-inch	common nails	
1 sheet	9x11 inches	100-grit sandpaper	
1 sheet	9x11 inches	220-grit sandpaper	
1 can	quart	primer	
1 can	quart	paint	

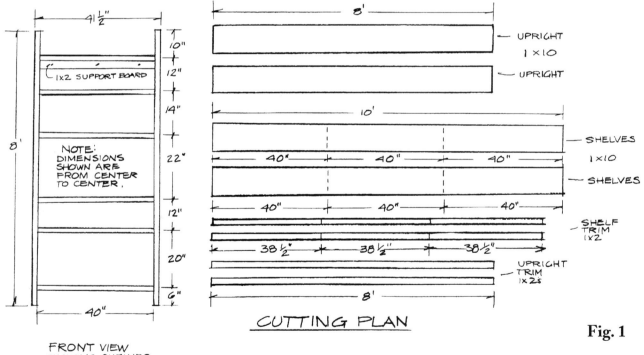

FRONT VIEW
SHOWING SHELVES
BEFORE 1X2 TRIM
IS APPLIED

CUTTING PLAN

Fig. 1

handsaw or a portable circular saw (see p. 26, Fig. 28B) to cut each shelf to a length of 40 inches, as shown in the Cutting Plan (see Fig. 1). Then stand them all together to make sure they are equal in length. If you have to remove a fraction of an inch and are using a handsaw, try this trick: Clamp a piece of scrap 1x10 over one end of the shelf board, mark where the cut should be and saw through both boards at once (see Fig. 3).

Lay the two uprights flat on the floor, side by side. Determine at what height you want each

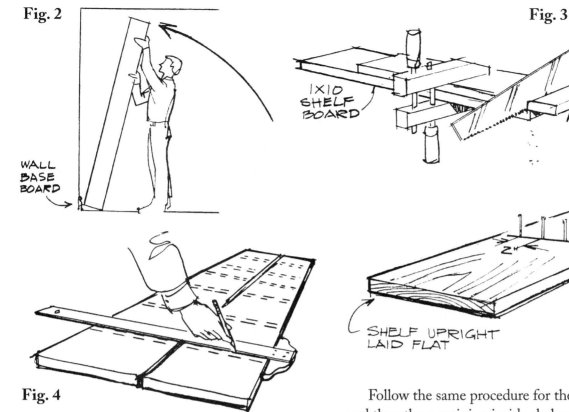

Fig. 2

WALL
BASE
BOARD

Fig. 3

1×10
SHELF
BOARD

SCRAP
BOARD

Fig. 4

Fig. 5

SHELF UPRIGHT
LAID FLAT

shelf. Lay a T-square flat across the two uprights and mark a pencil line across both of them where the center of each shelf will be located; continue the line around the edges of the uprights. Turn the boards over and make two parallel lines where the shelves will go, ¾ inch apart and ⅜ inch to either side of the single line on the two board edges (see Fig. 4).

To assemble the shelves, turn one of the uprights over so the single line shows and start four 2-inch finish nails, approximately 2 inches apart, on this line (see Fig. 5). Place the bottom shelf and the upright both on edge, fitting the shelf between the parallel lines on the inside of the upright. Brace the opposite end of the shelf against a solid surface, like a wall (see Fig. 6). Check that the other end of the shelf is perfectly aligned between the parallel lines and finish hammering in the nails.

Follow the same procedure for the top shelf, and then the remaining inside shelves. When you have all six shelves attached to one upright, turn the unit over and repeat the same procedure on the other side (see Fig. 7).

To make any necessary cuts in the uprights to accommodate a wall baseboard (see Fig. 8), lay the unit on its side and cut out the marked profile of the baseboard using an electric jigsaw (see p. 28, Fig. 32).

Stand up the unit and check with a level and square to make sure it is plumb. You may find that the shelving unit tips slightly forward. This is often the case on a wooden floor that has not been sanded as deeply and smoothly next to the wall. You can rectify this by taking the unit down and trimming the bottom end of the uprights at a slight slant (see Fig. 9).

As a safety precaution, to prevent the bookcase from falling forward and possibly causing injury, we suggest screwing it to the wall at the top.

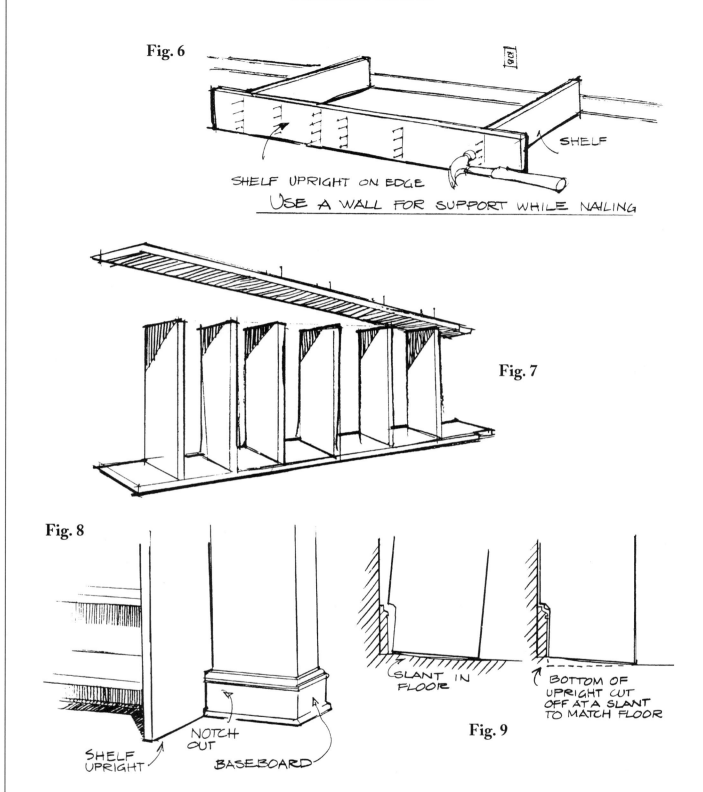

Fig. 6

SHELF

SHELF UPRIGHT ON EDGE

USE A WALL FOR SUPPORT WHILE NAILING

Fig. 7

Fig. 8

SHELF UPRIGHT

NOTCH OUT

BASEBOARD

SLANT IN FLOOR

BOTTOM OF UPRIGHT CUT OFF AT A SLANT TO MATCH FLOOR

Fig. 9

To do this, carefully measure and cut a support board out of 1x2 pine. Locate the wall studs (see p. 59), and screw through the support board and wall and into the studs (see Fig. 10). You can also attach the support board to the wall using wall anchors made for wallboard. Then hammer in at an angle one 3-inch finish nail every foot along the top shelf so that the nails penetrate the support board. This will secure the shelf to the wall (see Fig. 11).

Fig. 10

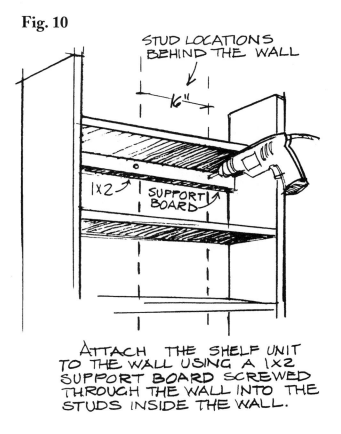

STUD LOCATIONS BEHIND THE WALL

16"

1x2   SUPPORT BOARD

ATTACH THE SHELF UNIT TO THE WALL USING A 1x2 SUPPORT BOARD SCREWED THROUGH THE WALL INTO THE STUDS INSIDE THE WALL.

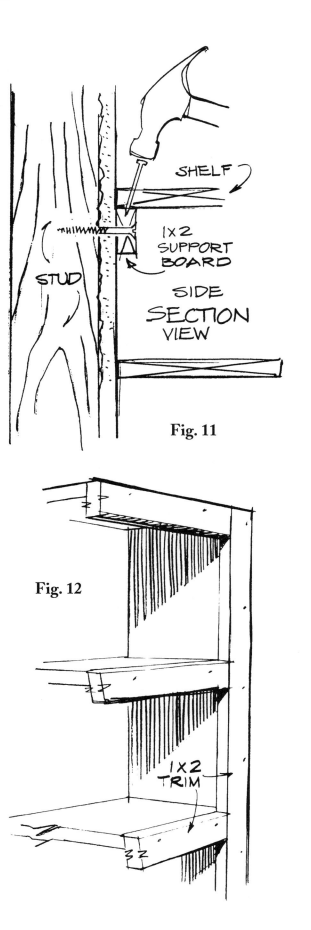

SHELF

THIMBLE

STUD

1x2 SUPPORT BOARD

SIDE SECTION VIEW

Fig. 11

Fig. 12

1x2 TRIM

3 2

To give the shelves a more finished look, cut two 1x2s to the same length as the uprights. Using 1½-inch finish nails spaced 6 inches apart, hammer the trim to the front edge of both uprights so that one edge overlaps the inside of the unit by ¾ inch and the other edge is flush with the outside of the upright. Next, cut two 10-foot lengths of 1x2 into six 38½-inch lengths, to trim the fronts of the shelves. Place the front trim flush with the top of each shelf, overlapping ¾ inch at the bottom (see Fig. 12), and secure it with 1½-inch finish nails spaced 6 inches apart.

Sand the shelves smooth, using 100-grit sandpaper, followed by 220-grit sandpaper, and a sanding block (see p. 53-54 and Figs. 78 and 79). Cover with a coat of primer, then paint the shelves a color of your choice.

Simple Shelf
WITH PEGS

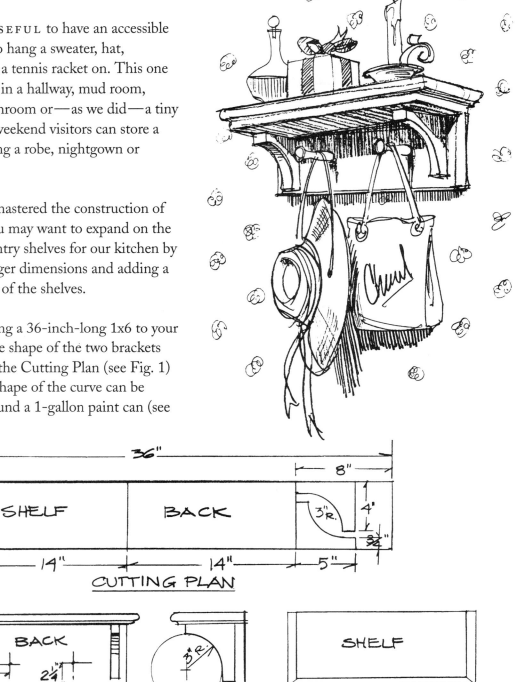

I T'S ALWAYS USEFUL to have an accessible shelf with pegs to hang a sweater, hat, umbrella or even a tennis racket on. This one is an ideal size to fit in a hallway, mud room, gardening shed, bathroom or—as we did—a tiny guest room, where weekend visitors can store a cosmetic kit and hang a robe, nightgown or pajamas.

Once you have mastered the construction of this simple shelf, you may want to expand on the design. We built pantry shelves for our kitchen by using wider and longer dimensions and adding a lip to the front edge of the shelves.

Begin by clamping a 36-inch-long 1x6 to your work table. Trace the shape of the two brackets onto the 1x6, using the Cutting Plan (see Fig. 1) as your guide. The shape of the curve can be made by tracing around a 1-gallon paint can (see

Fig. 1

36"

8"

5½"

SHELF   BACK   3"R.   4"

¾"

14"   14"   5"

CUTTING PLAN

BACK

3   2¼"

FRONT VIEW

3"R.

SIDE VIEW

SHELF

TOP VIEW

MATERIALS LIST

Quantity	Size	Description	Location or Use
2	14 inches	1x6 clear pine, cedar or cypress	shelf & back
2	4x5 inches	1x6 clear pine, cedar or cypress	brackets
1	36-inch strip	⅝ x ¾-inch nose & cove molding	
1 box	1½-inch	finish nails	
2-3	3-inch	Shaker pegs	back
2	3-inch	#10 drywall screws (or drywall anchors)	back
1 bottle	8 oz.	carpenter's glue	
1 sheet	9x11 inches	60-grit sandpaper	
1 sheet	9x11 inches	120-grit sandpaper	
1 sheet	9x11 inches	220-grit sandpaper	
1 can	10 oz.	water-based wood putty	

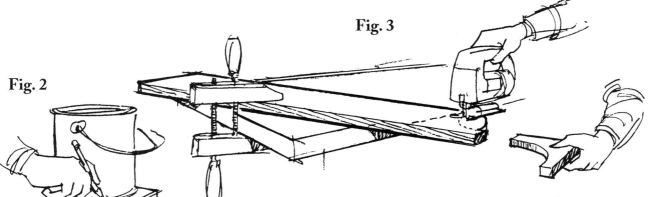

Fig. 3

Fig. 2

Fig. 2). Using an electric jigsaw (see p. 28, Fig. 32), cut out the two wooden brackets. **NOTE:** It's always best to cut off the smaller pieces of wood first, so that there's enough wood left to clamp onto (see Fig. 3).

Next, cut the two 14-inch-long pieces for the back and shelf. Wrap a piece of 60-grit sandpaper around a cylindrical object, such as a bottle or can, to smooth out any irregularities in the shape of the curve (see Fig. 4), then sand all the pieces with 120-grit sandpaper and a sanding block (see p. 53-54 and Figs. 78 and 79).

To avoid confusion later, make a light mark in pencil to identify which piece is the back, which is the shelf and which way the brackets are to be positioned.

Cover your work surface with newspaper and lay the front and back pieces on top. Squeeze a thin bead of glue down the center of the top edge of the back piece, and glue the underneath side of the shelf to this edge (see Fig. 5). Align both pieces so their side edges are flush with each other. If any glue seeps out onto the surface of the shelf, wipe it up immediately with a damp sponge, to avoid staining the wood. For a professional-looking job, use bar clamps to hold the two pieces together while the glue is drying (see p. 52,

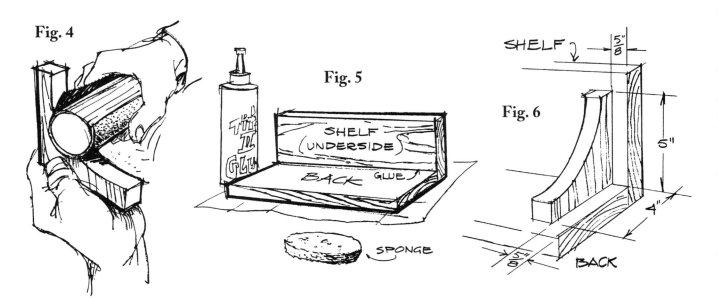

Fig. 4

Fig. 5

SHELF (UNDERSIDE)

BACK

GLUE

SPONGE

Fig. 6

SHELF

5/8"

5"

4"

5/8"

BACK

Fig. 7

BACK

SHELF

DRILL 1/16" PILOT HOLES FOR THE NAILS.

Fig. 8

5/8"

3/4"

NOSE & COVE MOLDING

Fig. 75). Before the glue has dried, temporarily hold the brackets in place to make sure that they will fit (see Fig. 6). Refer to the identification marks made earlier to double-check that the brackets are placed in the correct position. Then measure in ⅝ inch from each side of the shelf and back, and glue the two curved brackets in place. Allow the glue to dry overnight.

For extra strength, drill a total of twelve ¹⁄₁₆-inch pilot holes along the perimeter of the back and shelf pieces and into the brackets as shown (see Fig. 7). Don't drill too close to the ends of the brackets, as the nails might extend all the way through them. Hammer a 1½-inch-long finish nail into each hole.

For a more traditional look, we trimmed the edge of our shelf with a ⅝x¾-inch nose & cove molding (see Fig. 8). Cut the longest (front) piece of molding first. Hold the molding strip against the front edge of the shelf and make a mark where each corner of the shelf meets the molding. Use a combination square (see p. 22, Fig. 16) to mark a line at a 45-degree angle at each end (this will be your corner cut). With a handsaw and miter box or the saw guide described

Fig. 9

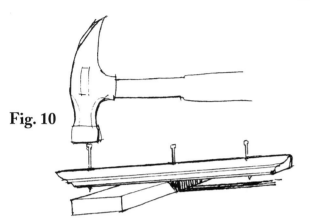

45° MITER CUT

SAW GUIDE

Fig. 10

½"

SHAKER PEG

Fig. 11

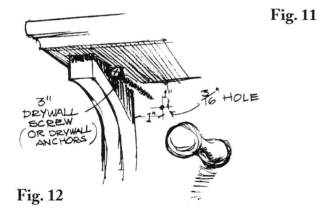

3" DRYWALL SCREW (OR DRYWALL ANCHORS)

3/16" HOLE

1"

Fig. 12

to make these 45-degree angled cuts. Carefully saw through the molding. When sawing the opposite end of the molding piece, slide the molding down and cut it with the saw blade placed on the *other* side of the saw guide.

You do *not* want the angled ends of the piece of molding to be parallel to each other. Use the same technique to cut the two molding pieces for the sides of the shelf. **NOTE:** It helps to draw your angled cut line on both sides of the molding, since making this simple cut can become very confusing!

Lay the front piece of molding on top of a piece of scrap wood and partially hammer in 1½-inch finish nails every 3 inches, until the points of the nails barely protrude through the back of the molding (see Fig. 10). Spread a thin bead of glue on the front edge of the shelf and carefully position the molding over the edge. After making sure both ends are correctly aligned, hammer the nails all the way in. Follow the same procedure for the two side pieces of molding, making sure to glue the ends of the molding as well. Sink the nails with a nail set (see p. 55, Fig. 85) and fill the holes with wood putty. After the putty dries, sand the wood smooth with 220-grit sandpaper.

For the pegs (see Fig. 11), drill two ½-inch-diameter holes 2¼ inches up from the bottom and 3 inches in from the brackets, going ⅝ inch deep. With a toothpick or a small stick of wood, spread some glue in the hole and twist the peg in.

To hang the shelf, drill two 3/16-inch holes in the upper left and right corners of the back piece, measuring 1 inch in from the bracket and 1 inch down from the underneath side of the shelf. Secure the shelf to the wall with 3-inch #10 drywall screws or drywall anchors (see Fig. 12).

on p. 63, cut the molding pieces. When using the saw guide, always place the flat top side of the molding face-down on the saw guide surface, with the curved side facing inward toward the fence. Position the molding in the saw guide, lining up your pencil mark with the diagonal slot on the saw guide (see Fig. 9). A fine-toothed saw works best

Slatted Stool
OR END TABLE

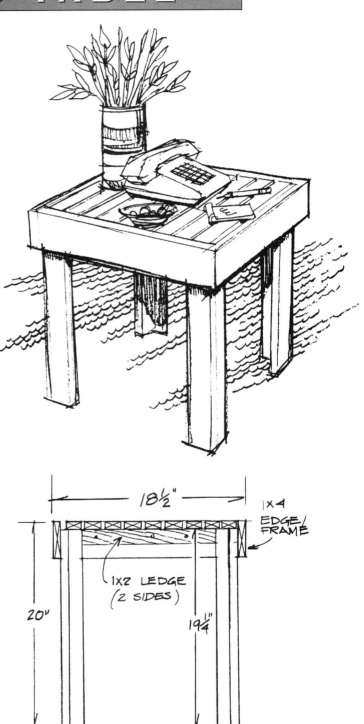

THIS FUNCTIONAL piece of furniture can serve as a stool or as an end or side table. It is a classic design, appealing both inside the house or outside on a deck or porch. For indoor use, we recommend using pine; for outdoors, a rot-resistant wood such as cypress, redwood or cedar works best.

Fairly simple to build, this project uses stock lumber and requires no fancy cuts. All of the cuts can be easily made using the saw guide described on p. 63.

Since clear white pine is three times as expensive as #2 common pine, we've found that it's more economical to buy long lengths of #2 pine and cut the pieces out of the clear sections of the lumber. When you are at the lumberyard picking out your materials, give yourself plenty of time to locate pieces that are as knot-free as possible.

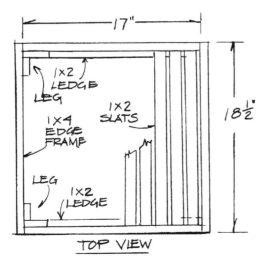

17"

1X2 LEDGE

LEG

1X2 SLATS

1X4 EDGE FRAME

LEG

1X2 LEDGE

18½"

TOP VIEW

18½"

1X4 EDGE FRAME

1X2 LEDGE (2 SIDES)

20"

19¼"

SECTION
SIDE VIEW

MATERIALS LIST

Quantity	Size	Description	Location or Use
2	17 inches	1x4 #2 common pine	edge/frame
2	18½ inches	1x4 #2 common pine	edge/frame
4	19¼ inches	1x3 #2 common pine	legs
4	19¼ inches	1x2 #2 common pine	legs
2	12 inches	1x2 #2 common pine	support ledges
9	17 inches	1x2 #2 common pine	top slats
1 box	1¼-inch	galvanized finish nails	
14	1¼-inch	#8 galvanized deck screws	support ledges
8	2-inch	#10 Phillips-head screws	
8	⅜-inch-dia. x ¼-inch	wood plugs	
1 bottle	8 oz.	Titebond II glue	
1 can	10 oz.	wood putty	
1 sheet	9x11 inches	60-grit sandpaper	
1 sheet	9x11 inches	120-grit sandpaper	
1 can	quart	stain, paint or wood sealer	

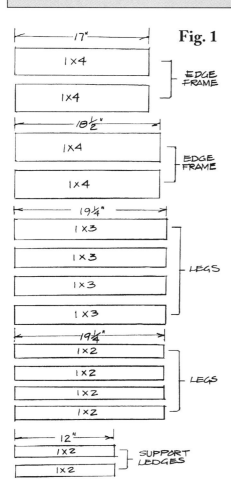

Fig. 1

CUTTING PLAN

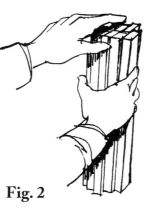

Fig. 2

Begin by measuring, marking and cutting out the eight leg pieces, one at a time (see Cutting Plan, Fig. 1). Each leg is made up of two pieces, a 1x3 and a 1x2, which are butted up against each other, forming a leg corner. Use the saw guide and a handsaw to cut four 1x3s and four 1x2s, each 19¼ inches long. If you do not have a saw guide, clamp the wood securely to your work table and measure, mark and cut the lengths carefully with a handsaw. Check to see if the legs are identical lengths by standing them up together on end (see Fig. 2). If they aren't, use 60-grit sandpaper and a sanding block (see p. 53-54 and Figs. 78 and 79) to sand off any discrepancies in length.

NOTE: Because the tops of the legs will be hidden by the frame of the table, perfect cuts are not as important as they are with the 1x4 edge/frame pieces and the tabletop slats, which *are* visible and need to be as accurate as possible.

Assemble the four legs by gluing and nailing the 1x3 pieces to the 1x2 pieces. Hammer three 1¼-inch galvanized finish nails, equally spaced, through a 1x3 and into the edge of a 1x2. To support the pieces while you are assembling them, place a scrap piece of 1x2 on edge under the 1x3 (see Fig. 3). Repeat this procedure for the other three legs.

Fig. 3

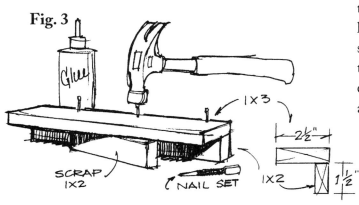

Use a nail set (see Fig. 3 and p. 55, Fig. 85) to sink all the nail heads below the surface of the wood. Fill the holes with wood putty. When the putty has dried, sand the legs with 60-grit and then 120-grit sandpaper and a sanding block.

The four table legs will be attached to a 1x4 frame. To make the frame, use a saw guide and a handsaw to carefully cut two 1x4 edge/frame pieces, both 17 inches long, and two 1x4 edge/frame pieces, both 18½ inches long. Again, if you are not using a saw guide, securely clamp the wood to your work table, and carefully measure, mark and cut the four pieces. Since these corner joints will be clearly visible on the top of the table, they should be cut as accurately as possible. After cutting the four pieces, sand them with 60-grit sandpaper, followed by 120-grit sandpaper.

Fig. 4

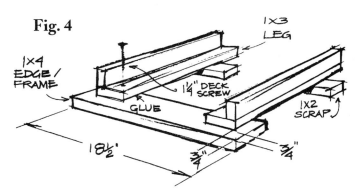

To attach the legs to the edge/frame, lay one of the 18½-inch long 1x4s face down on your work surface and place a leg at both ends, leaving a ¾-inch space above and to the side of each leg (see Fig. 4). Put a scrap 1x2 (or other ¾-inch-thick wood) under the free end of both legs to keep them level. Glue the 1x3 to the 1x4, and screw one 1¼-inch galvanized deck screw into the top center of each 1x3 and into the 1x4 edge/frame. Check to make sure the ¾-inch allowances are accurate by testing them with a scrap piece of 1x4. Without waiting for the glue to dry, repeat the same procedure for the remaining two legs and edge/frame.

To join the two leg sets together, lay one of the 17-inch-long 1x4 edge/frame pieces down on your work surface. Tipping the two leg sets on their sides (see Fig. 5), position the 17-inch edge/frame piece so that it fits into the ¾-inch space at the ends of the leg sets. Glue the wood together, then drill one 1¼-inch screw through the top of each 1x2 leg and into the 17-inch edge/frame, once again allowing for the ¾-inch recesses. Turn the assembled unit over on its opposite side and repeat the process.

For a first-rate look, use a ⅜-inch spade bit (see p. 49, Fig. 70) to counterbore two ⅜-inch-diameter ¼-inch-deep holes into each end of each of the two overlapping (18½-inch-long) 1x4s, measuring ⅜ inch in from each side (see Fig. 5). Screw the corners together using 2-inch Phillips-head screws and fill the ⅜-inch holes

Fig. 5

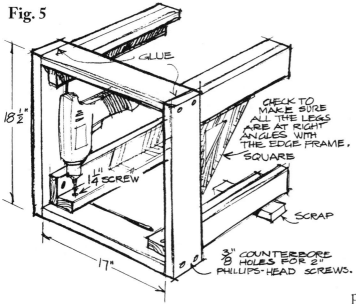

Fig. 7

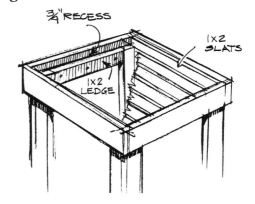

with either wood putty or ⅜-inch-diameter wood plugs (see p. 49, Fig. 69).

Before the glue has dried, check to make sure the legs are at right angles to the top by placing a square where the legs meet the top. The legs have a tendency to bend in slightly, but this can be corrected by placing temporary diagonal supports approximately 21½ inches long between the legs while the glue is drying (see Fig. 6).

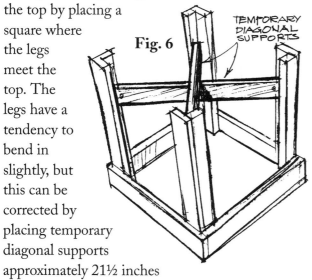

Fig. 6

The tabletop consists of nine slats supported by two ledges. To make the ledge pieces, use the saw guide and handsaw to cut two pieces of 1x2, each 12 inches long. Position one ledge piece between two 1x3 leg sections and ¾ inch down

from the top of the edge/frame piece, allowing a ¾-inch space for the slats. Position the other ledge between the opposite pair of 1x3 leg sections, again leaving a ¾-inch space for the slats. Attach each support ledge using three 1¼-inch galvanized deck screws placed approximately 3 inches apart (see Figs. 4 and 7).

Measure and cut nine pieces of 1x2 #2 pine, each exactly 17 inches long. Check to see if the slats are identical lengths by standing them up on end. Use 60-grit sandpaper and a sanding block to sand off any irregular ends.

Before gluing the slats to the ledge and frame of the table, temporarily lay them in place, resting them on the support ledges. Mark with a pencil where each one will eventually be positioned. Make sure each slat is smooth by sanding first with 60-grit sandpaper and a sanding block, followed by 120-grit sandpaper. Glue the slats to the inside of the edge frame and the 1x2 ledge, allowing approximately ⅜-inch gap between each slat.

We finished our pine table by wiping it with a white stain and then applying two coats of polyurethane. This wood also looks nice painted with two coats of glossy white enamel. If you build the table out of redwood, cypress or cedar and plan to use it outdoors, seal the wood with a clear wood sealer, such as Thompson's Waterseal, to make it more impervious to the elements.

Work or Potting
B E N C H

THIS UTILITY BENCH can serve many purposes, ranging from woodworking to household repairs to gardening projects. It requires only straight cuts, and can easily be built on a Saturday morning. We suggest attaching it to a wall with lag screws to make it sturdy and secure enough for carpentry projects.

The work surface consists of 2x6 fir boards that overhang two sides by 3 inches, enabling you to clamp boards to the top of it. The bottom shelf is deep enough to hold large items, storing them out of the way while keeping them visible and accessible. The top ledge provides a convenient place for chisels, screwdrivers, drill bits, trowels, clippers and other small hand tools that are used frequently.

Begin by building the two leg sets. The leg pieces for *each* leg set can be cut from one 10-foot-long 2x4, and *all* the top and bottom cross supports for both sides can be cut from one 10-foot-long 2x4. Consequently, you will need to buy a total of three 10-foot-long 2x4s.

MATERIALS LIST

Quantity	Size	Description	Location or Use
5	54 inches	2x6 fir	tabletop
4	30½ inches	2x4 fir	legs
4	17½ inches	2x4 fir	legs
4	6 inches	2x4 fir	legs
2	27 inches	2x4 fir	top cross supports
2	24 inches	2x4 fir	bottom cross supports
3	48 inches	1x6 #2 common pine	bottom shelf
1	54 inches	1x12 #2 common pine	backboard
1	54 inches	1x3 #2 common pine	top ledge
1 box	2½-inch	#10 galvanized deck screws	
1 box	1½-inch	#8 galvanized deck screws	
20	½-inch-dia. x ¼-inch	wood plugs	
1 belt	6x48-inch	40-grit sandpaper	tabletop
1 belt	6x48-inch	60-grit sandpaper	tabletop
1 sheet	9x11 inches	60-grit sandpaper	top ledge

Refer to the Cutting Plan (see Fig. 1) as you cut out the individual pieces. Rest the first 2x4 on top of two sawhorses or a work surface. Use a tape measure and pencil to mark the first 6-inch-long leg piece, draw a cut line with a combination square (see p. 22, Fig. 15) and saw the piece off where marked, using a handsaw or a portable circular saw. Measure, mark and cut each of the leg pieces separately, using the same procedure. You will be cutting two 6-inch, two 17½-inch and two 30½-inch pieces from two of the 10-foot 2x4s. After all the leg pieces have been cut, measure, mark and cut the two 27-inch top and the two 24-inch bottom cross supports out of the third 10-foot 2x4.

One at a time, clamp each of the two 27-inch cross support pieces to a sturdy work surface and use a combination square to mark a 45-degree angle ½ inch down from the corner of the top cross support. Use a handsaw to cut off the piece, so that the bottom of the cut is 3 inches in from the end of the top cross support (see Fig. 2).

After all the pieces that make up the leg sets are cut to size, temporarily assemble them on the floor, laying them side by side (see Fig. 3). **NOTE:** It is important when you assemble the leg sets to make sure that the cross supports of each set will face *inside* the bench once it is built.

After you have checked to see that the leg assemblies fit together, use a VSR electric drill with a Phillips screwdriver bit to screw together all eight pieces of each leg set with 2½-inch galvanized deck screws. Space the screws approximately 5 inches apart and stagger them, placing two in each bottom section of the leg and three in each top section.

To make the bottom shelf, cut three 48-inch-long pieces out of one 12-foot-long piece of 1x6 #2 pine. Stand the two leg sets up with the help of an assistant (or prop them up against a wall if

Fig. 1

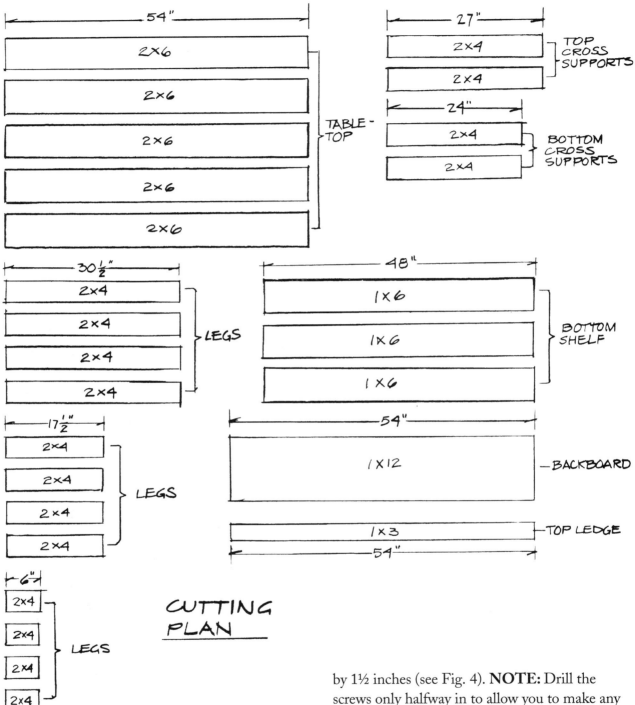

CUTTING
PLAN

by 1½ inches (see Fig. 4). **NOTE:** Drill the screws only halfway in to allow you to make any necessary adjustments before the workbench is completed.

To make the tabletop pieces, cut five pieces of 2x6 fir, each 54 inches long. Temporarily screw one of these boards across the front of

you are alone) and use a Phillips screwdriver to temporarily screw the three 1x6 bottom shelf pieces to the bottom cross supports, so that the ends of the shelf boards overhang the crossbraces

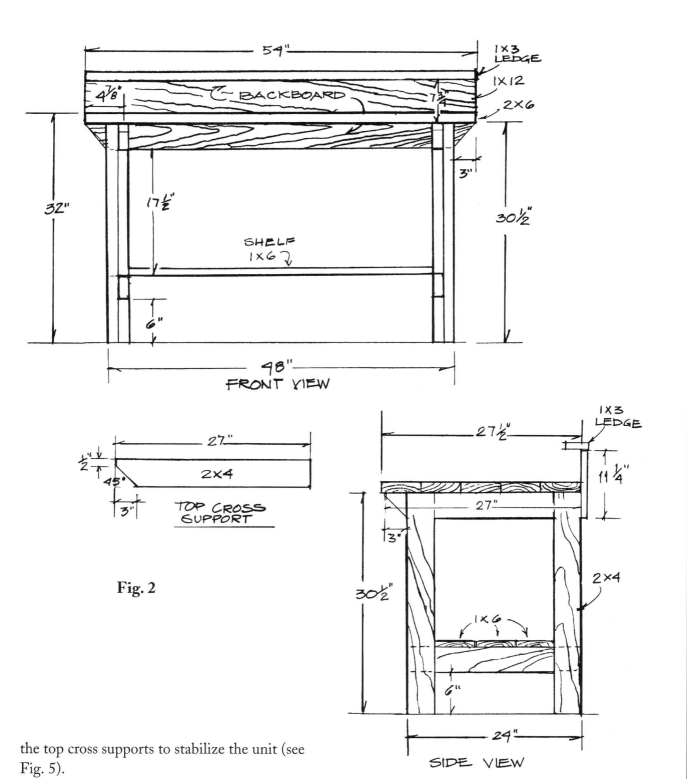

54"

1X3
LEDGE

4⅞"

BACKBOARD

1X12

7¾"

2X6

32"

17½"

30½"

3"

SHELF
1X6

6"

48"

FRONT VIEW

27"

½"

2X4

45°

3"

TOP CROSS
SUPPORT

Fig. 2

1X3
LEDGE

27½"

11¼"

27"

3"

30½"

1X6

2X4

6"

24"

SIDE VIEW

the top cross supports to stabilize the unit (see Fig. 5).

Next, make the backboard by cutting one piece of 1x12 #2 pine 54 inches long. Temporarily hold the backboard in position by placing two screws through the backboard and into the back of the legs (see Fig. 4). The backboard should ex-

tend 7¾ inches above the top of the cross supports. Place a mark 7¾ inches down from each top corner of the backboard and mark a diagonal line from this point to where the backboard meets the legs (approximately a 45-degree angle).

LEG SETS

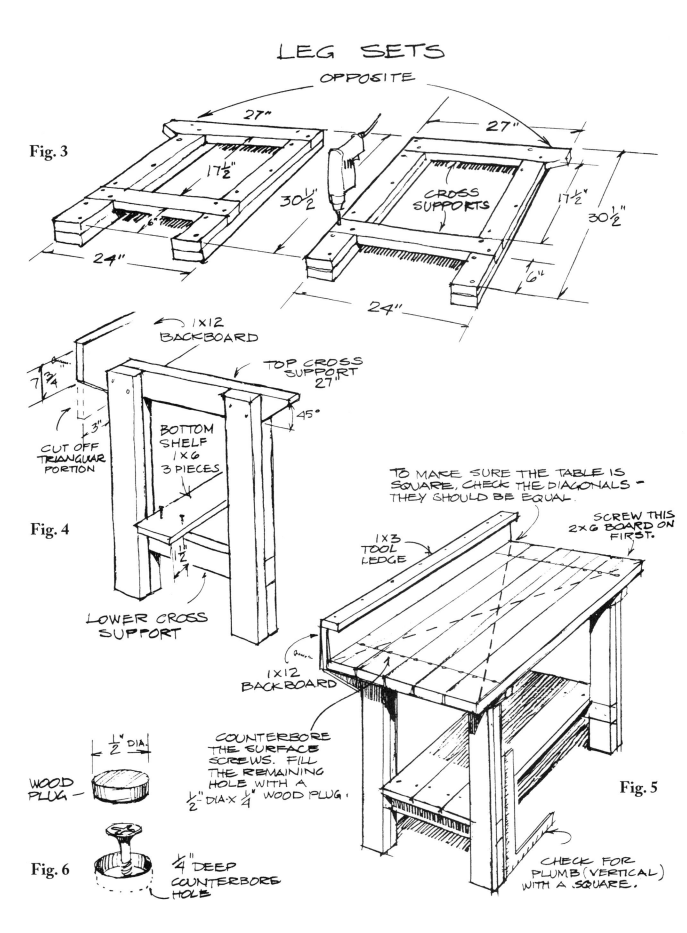

OPPOSITE

Fig. 3

27"

17½"

30½"

24"

CROSS SUPPORTS

27"

17½"

30½"

6"

24"

7¾"

3"

CUT OFF TRIANGULAR PORTION

1x12 BACKBOARD

TOP CROSS SUPPORT 27"

45°

BOTTOM SHELF 1x6 3 PIECES

Fig. 4

½"

LOWER CROSS SUPPORT

TO MAKE SURE THE TABLE IS SQUARE, CHECK THE DIAGONALS — THEY SHOULD BE EQUAL.

SCREW THIS 2x6 BOARD ON FIRST.

1x3 TOOL LEDGE

1x12 BACKBOARD

COUNTERBORE THE SURFACE SCREWS. FILL THE REMAINING HOLE WITH A ½"-DIA.x ¼" WOOD PLUG.

Fig. 5

½" DIA.

WOOD PLUG

Fig. 6

¼" DEEP COUNTERBORE HOLE

CHECK FOR PLUMB (VERTICAL) WITH A SQUARE.

Remove the backboard and cut this triangular section off each end.

Screw the backboard on again, using the same temporary screw holes. Before going on to the next step, use a framing square to check that the unit is plumb (vertically straight) and square (see Fig. 5). Make sure that the legs line up at right angles with the floor and the bottom and top shelves. Check the top work surface by measuring the diagonals with a tape measure: They should be the same length (see Fig. 5). If the tabletop is not square, make adjustments by twisting it into the correct position.

Position the four remaining 2x6 tabletop boards on top of the two crosspieces so that their ends are lined up evenly. Make sure that there is an equal amount of space between each board. To mark where you should place your screw holes, measure in 4⅞ inches from each side of the tabletop, and using a framing square as your guide, draw a line from back to front. Make sure that the lines are over the center of each cross support (see Fig. 5). Use a ½-inch spade bit to counterbore ¼-inch-deep holes for the screws (see Figs. 5 and 6 and p. 49, Fig. 70). This will prevent the screw heads in the work surface from marring anything placed on top of it. Drill 2½-inch-long #10 galvanized deck screws through each hole and into the cross supports. Screw eight 1½-inch #8 screws, equally spaced, through the backboard and into the tabletop edge. Tighten all the screws. Fill the screw holes in the work surface with ½-inch-diameter by ¼-inch-thick wood plugs (see Fig. 6). Sand the tabletop surface *across* the grain, using a belt sander (see p. 55, Fig. 83) fitted with 40-grit sandpaper.

To make the top tool ledge, cut a piece of 1x3 to measure 54 inches long, and screw it to the top of the 1x12 backboard with 1½-inch #8 galvanized deck screws, spaced 6 inches apart (see Fig. 5). Lay the hand tools that you expect to use most often on the tabletop and mark on the 1x3 where they should go. Some tools, such as drill bits and screwdrivers, need only a hole drilled, while others, like pliers and chisels, require notches to be cut out of the front of the tool shelf to hold them (see Fig. 7). Use a ½-inch spade bit to drill holes for the notches. Cut out the material in front of the hole with an electric jigsaw. Make sure that each notch or hole is at least 1½ inches on-center from the next hole. To make the holes, use a ¼-inch spade bit. Sand the inside of the notches and holes with a rolled-up piece of 60-grit sandpaper (see p. 83, Fig. 11).

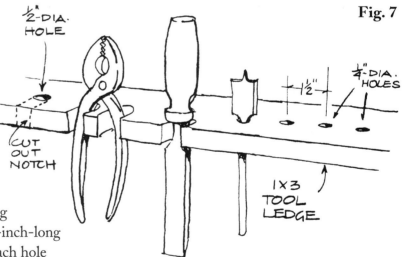

Fig. 7

To finish the work surface and make it perfectly level, sand *with* the grain, using a belt sander fitted with 60-grit sandpaper. This project does not need to be coated with wood sealer, paint or stain.

Herb
RACK

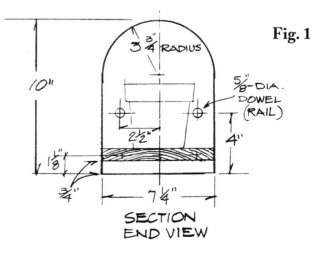

LIGHTWEIGHT AND SIMPLE in design, this herb rack requires only a minimal amount of wood. It is an ideal size for a kitchen window and easy to transport from one room to another or even take outside once spring arrives.

We built ours out of clear cedar, but you can also use other rot-resistant woods, such as redwood, teak or cypress. Since it comes in contact with a lot of dirt and water, and may be moved outside, it's a good idea to give the herb rack a few coats of clear wood sealer such as Thompson's Waterseal.

When a number of pieces of wood are being cut from the same board, it's advisable to cut the smaller ones first, so you have enough board left

over to clamp firmly to your work surface. So this project begins with the two curved 10-inch end pieces (see Fig. 1). Clamp the 39-inch-long board to your work table and draw a curve with a 3¾-inch radius, using a compass placed at the center

Fig. 1

10"

3¾ RADIUS

5/8"-DIA. DOWEL (RAIL)

2½"

4"

1⅛"

¾"

7¼"

SECTION END VIEW

112

MATERIALS LIST

Quantity	Size	Description	Location or Use
2	10 inches	1x8 clear cedar	ends
1	19 inches	1x8 clear cedar	bottom
2	21 inches	⅝-inch-dia. dowel	rails
6	2-inch	#8 Phillips-head screws	
1 sheet	9x11 inches	60-grit sandpaper	
1 sheet	9x11 inches	120-grit sandpaper	
1 sheet	9x11 inches	220-grit sandpaper	
6	½-inch-dia. x ¼-inch	wood plugs	
1 can	10 oz.	wood putty	
1 can	quart	wood sealer	
1	3 feet	⅝-inch-dia. white nylon rope (optional)	
2	2½-inch	#6 ceiling hooks (optional)	

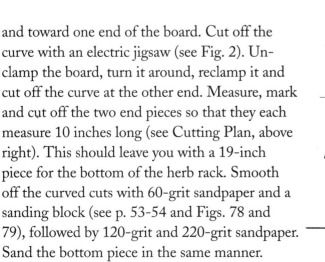

Next, drill two holes in both end pieces where the rails will be placed. To do this, measure and mark a vertical line down the center of each end piece. Then measure and mark 4 inches up from the bottom and 2½ inches away from the centerline on both end pieces (see Fig. 1).

Fig. 2

and toward one end of the board. Cut off the curve with an electric jigsaw (see Fig. 2). Unclamp the board, turn it around, reclamp it and cut off the curve at the other end. Measure, mark and cut off the two end pieces so that they each measure 10 inches long (see Cutting Plan, above right). This should leave you with a 19-inch piece for the bottom of the herb rack. Smooth off the curved cuts with 60-grit sandpaper and a sanding block (see p. 53-54 and Figs. 78 and 79), followed by 120-grit and 220-grit sandpaper. Sand the bottom piece in the same manner.

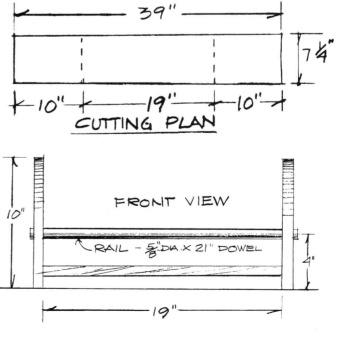

Lay one end piece on top of a piece of scrap wood on the floor, hold the wood down with your foot and drill halfway through the end piece, using a ⅝-inch spade bit (see Fig. 3). Turn the end piece over and continue drilling through the other side until the drill goes all the way through. Do the same for the second hole. Repeat the entire procedure on the other end piece.

Fig. 3

SCRAP BOARD

Cut two pieces of ⅝-inch-diameter dowel 21 inches long using an electric jigsaw. Twist the two dowels through the holes so their ends protrude slightly through the outside of the end pieces (see p. 113, Front View).

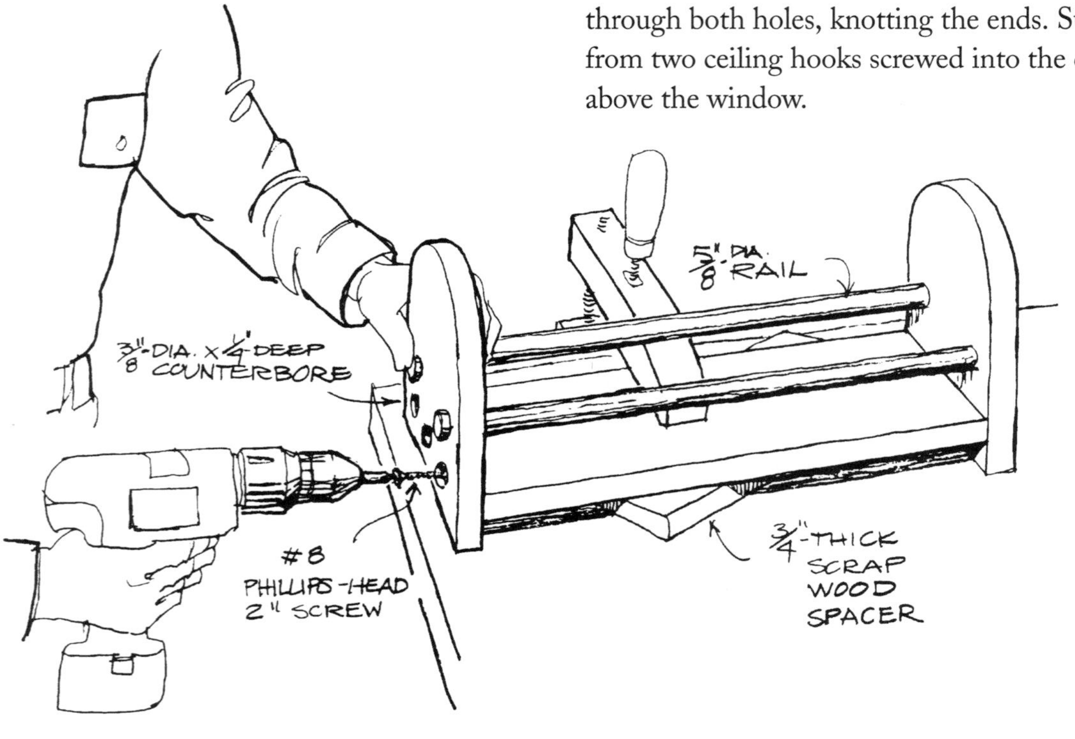

To attach the ends to the base, use a ⅜-inch spade bit to drill three ⅜-inch-diameter counterbore holes at each end. The holes should be ¼ inch deep, 2½ inches apart and 1⅛ inch up from the bottom of each end piece.

Place a scrap piece of ¾-inch-thick wood under the 19-inch-long base piece to act as a spacer and clamp the base and spacer to the workbench. Place one end piece flush against the end of the bottom piece and drill three 2-inch #8 Phillips-head screws through the counterbored holes and into the base piece (see Fig. 4). Repeat for the other end. Fill the holes with either wood putty or ½-inch-diameter wood plugs (see p. 49, Fig. 69).

Give all surfaces a final sanding using 220-grit sandpaper and a sanding block. Seal with two coats of wood sealer.

This herb rack can easily be adapted to hang in a window. Drill a ⅝-inch-diameter hole in both end pieces near the top and thread a 3-foot-long piece of ⅝-inch-diameter white nylon rope through both holes, knotting the ends. Suspend it from two ceiling hooks screwed into the casing above the window.

Fig. 4

⅜" DIA. X ¼" DEEP COUNTERBORE

#8 PHILLIPS-HEAD 2" SCREW

⅝" DIA. RAIL

¾"-THICK SCRAP WOOD SPACER

Picket
PLANTER

ORTABLE AND VERSATILE, this
lightweight planter can be placed in front
of a window until spring arrives, then
moved outdoors to a deck or porch. It is designed
to hold pots with a 6-inch diameter or less.

The handmade pickets are somewhat labor-
intensive, but using an electric jigsaw simplifies
the task. Once you have finished cutting out the
pickets, the rest of the planter goes together
quickly.

Using a handsaw with either a miter box or a
saw guide (see p. 63), cut the eight 1x2 rail pieces
from one 12-foot-long piece of #2 pine. The four
side rails should each be 25 inches long, and the
four end rails should each be 7¼ inches long (see
Cutting Plan, Fig. 1).

From two 12-foot lengths of ¼x1½-inch
lattice molding, cut 30 pieces, each 8½ inches
long. Then trace the picket profile (see Fig. 2)
onto a piece of cardboard (the back of pads of
paper or cardboard from dry-cleaned shirts works
great). Cut out this template and use it to trace
the picket shape onto both sides of the 30 pieces
of lattice. **NOTE:** By marking the shape on both
sides, you will always be sawing away from the
hand holding the piece of wood.

Either clamp one end of a picket to your
workbench or use one hand to hold it firmly in
place. Using an electric jigsaw and sawing away
from the hand holding the picket, cut one side,
turn the picket over, and cut the other side (see
Fig. 3).

MATERIALS LIST

Quantity	Size	Description	Location or Use
4	7¼ inches	1x2 #2 common pine	end rails
4	25 inches	1x2 #2 common pine	side rails
1	25 inches	1x8 #2 cedar	bottom
4	12 inches	2x2 clear cedar	legs
30	8½ inches	¼x1½-inch lattice molding	pickets
1 box	1-inch	galvanized wire nails	pickets
1 box	2-inch	galvanized finish nails	
12	2½-inch	galvanized finish nails	legs
1 bottle	8 oz.	carpenter's glue	
1 can	10 oz.	water-based wood putty	
1 sheet	9x11 inches	60-grit sandpaper	
1 sheet	9x11 inches	120-grit sandpaper	
1 can	quart	white gloss enamel paint	

Fig. 1

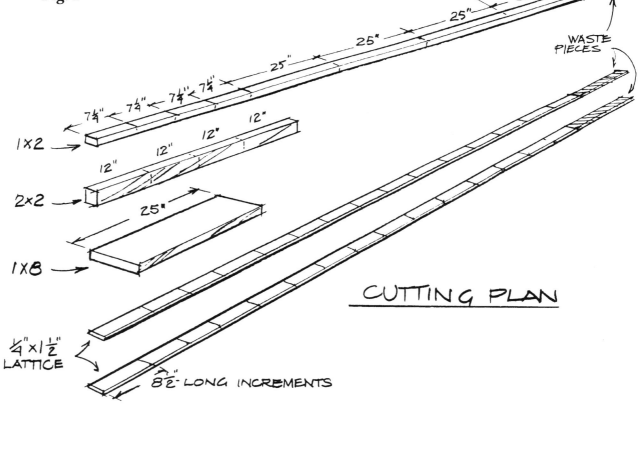

CUTTING PLAN

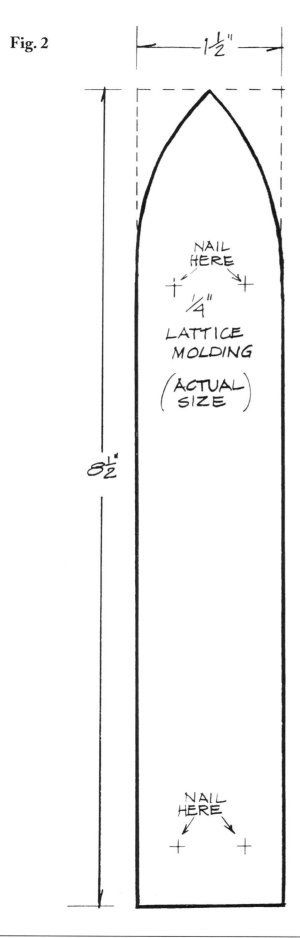

Fig. 2

1½"

NAIL
HERE

¼"

LATTICE
MOLDING

(ACTUAL
SIZE)

8½"

NAIL
HERE

Fig. 3

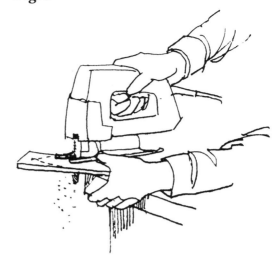

Lay two of the 25-inch-long rail pieces on your work table so they are exactly 4 inches apart. To keep the rails from moving while you are gluing the pickets in place, hammer two 1-inch galvanized wire nails, one at one end of each of the two rails, temporarily attaching them to your work table. Space the pickets approximately ½ inch apart, placing two small dots of carpenter's glue on the back of each one and laying them on top of the rail pieces. Use a piece of ½-inch-thick scrap wood to measure the space between each picket (see Fig. 4). You may have to make some adjustments on either end. Follow the same procedure for the three remaining sides, checking as you go along to make sure that the overall height of the rails always measures 7 inches. Use a combination square (see p. 22, Fig. 15) to check periodically that you are gluing the pickets on straight, as it's easy to get them out of alignment. By gluing them first, you can make adjustments before hammering in the nails. After the glue dries, hammer two, equally spaced, 1-inch galvanized wire nails at the top and bottom of each picket and into the rails. Use a nail set (see p. 55, Fig. 85) to sink the nails, and lightly sand the pickets with 60-grit sandpaper and a sanding block (see p. 53-54 and Figs. 78 and 79), followed by 120-grit sandpaper.

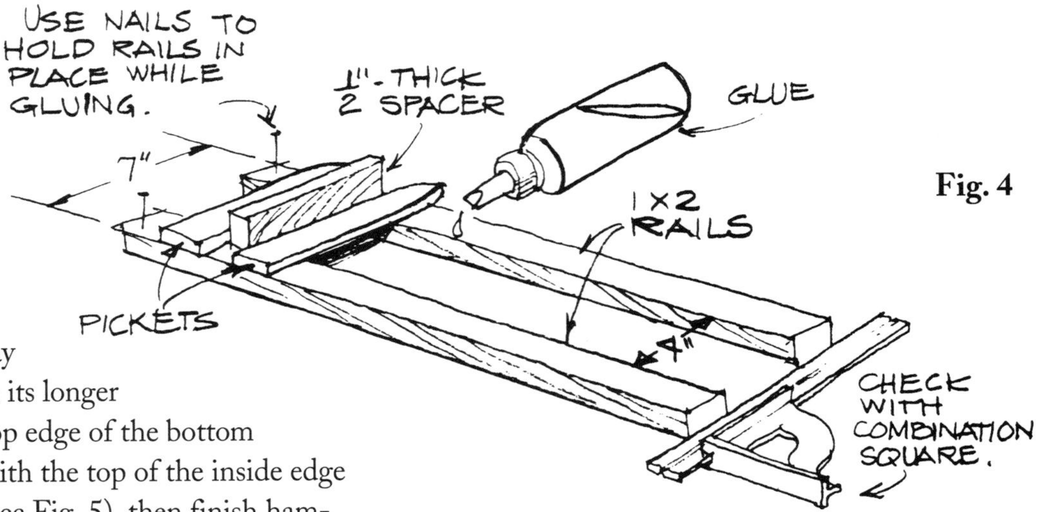

To join the picket fence to the bottom piece, first partially hammer 2-inch finish nails into every other picket where the pickets are attached to the bottom rail. Then lay the bottom piece on its longer edge. Line up the top edge of the bottom piece so it is flush with the top of the inside edge of the bottom rail (see Fig. 5), then finish hammering the nails through the picket, rail and bottom piece. Continue turning the base/picket unit over, attaching the three other sides in the same manner. Make sure to "start" the nails first, then align the picket fence with the bottom piece and finish hammering in the nails.

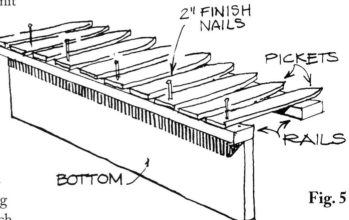

Fig. 4

Construct the four corner posts or legs of the picket planter last. Cut four pieces of 2x2, each 10½ inches long. Make a pencil mark 1¾ inches up from the bottom of each leg. Starting with one side, glue two legs into the rails at each corner of the planter, so the rails are 1¾ inches up from the bottom of the legs (see Fig. 6). Use a toothpick or flat stick to spread the glue evenly over the exposed ends, wiping off any excess with a damp sponge.

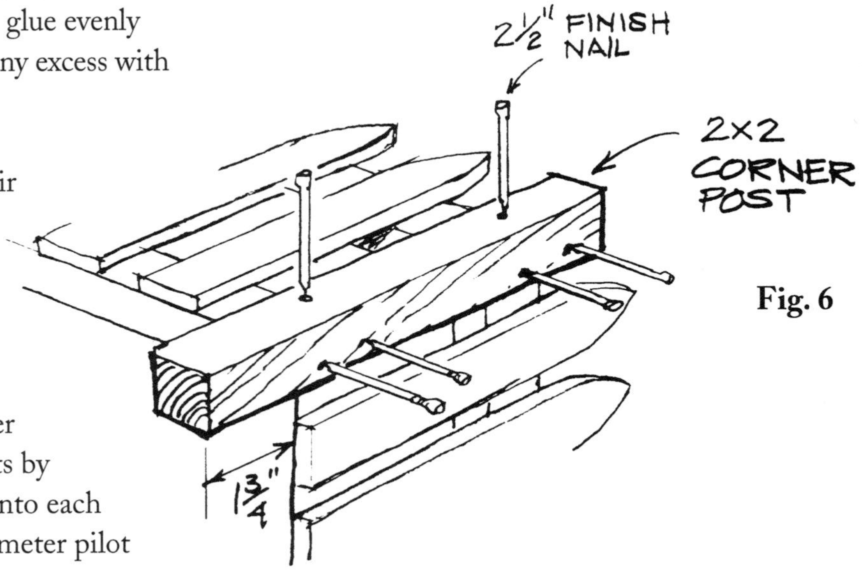

Fig. 5

When positioning the legs, their tops should be the same height (or slightly higher) than the tops of the pickets. If you have bar clamps (see p. 52, Fig. 75), use them to hold the legs to the picket fence while the glue is drying. After the glue is dry, strengthen the joints by nailing three 2½-inch finish nails into each one (see Fig. 6). Drill ¹⁄₁₆-inch-diameter pilot

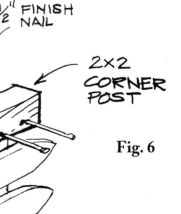

Fig. 6

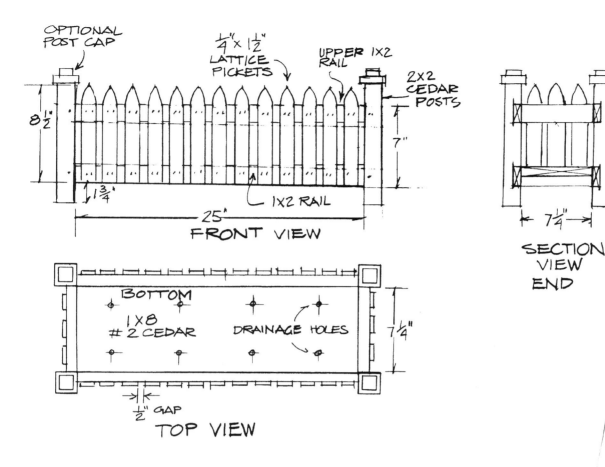

OPTIONAL POST CAP

$\frac{1}{4}" \times 1\frac{1}{2}"$ LATTICE PICKETS

UPPER RAIL 1X2

2X2 CEDAR POSTS

$8\frac{1}{2}"$

7"

$1\frac{3}{4}"$

1X2 RAIL

25"

FRONT VIEW

BOTTOM

$\frac{1}{X8}$ #2 CEDAR

DRAINAGE HOLES

$7\frac{1}{4}"$

$\frac{1}{2}"$ GAP

TOP VIEW

$10\frac{1}{2}"$

$7\frac{1}{4}"$

SECTION VIEW END

holes for the nails and stagger them, two in the sides and one in the front, so the nails will not meet inside the legs. Set the nails deep into the wood and plug the nail holes with wood putty. Drill eight ½-inch-diameter drainage holes in the bottom piece, equidistant apart, to allow for drainage (see Top View, above). After sanding with 60-grit and 120-grit sandpaper and a sanding block, give the planter three coats of white gloss enamel paint.

If you are feeling creative, decorate the tops of the posts with finials or design something yourself, using scrap pieces of wood.

Bluebird

HOUSE

SYMBOLS OF LOVE, hope and good fortune, bluebirds are excellent birds to attract to your garden. They are beautiful songbirds and are also beneficial to gardens because they dine on many of the insects that are destructive to flowers and vegetables.

Bluebirds are very particular about the size of the entrance hole to their house. It should be *exactly* 1½ inches in diameter for the eastern bluebird and 1⁹⁄₁₆ inches in diameter for mountain and western bluebirds. Our first bluebird house remained empty all year until we discovered that a squirrel had gained access by nibbling its way around the hole, enlarging it to an unacceptable 3 inches.

Ventilation is another important requirement. We have designed this bluebird house so the sides do not reach up all the way to the roof, allowing a small crack for fresh air. Painting the birdhouse is not necessary, and in fact may discourage bluebirds from moving in.

Bluebirds prefer houses that are placed on poles, protected from squirrels, or in trees that grow on the edge of a clearing. Though bluebirds can be difficult to entice, once you have won them over, they will thrive and add a new dimension to your garden.

Fig. 1

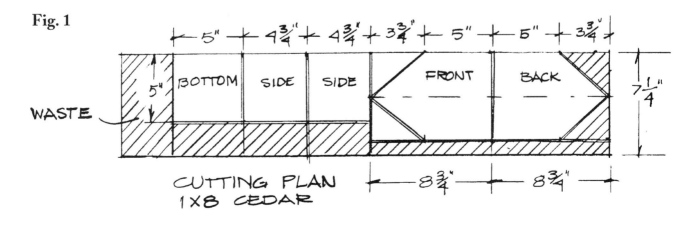

MATERIALS LIST

Quantity	Size	Description	Location or Use
2	6½x8¾ inches	1x8 #2 cedar, cypress or redwood	front, back
2	4¾x5 inches	1x8 #2 cedar, cypress or redwood	sides
1	5x5 inches	1x8 #2 cedar, cypress or redwood	bottom
4	9x6 inches	red cedar shingles	roof
1	8 feet	1⅜-inch-dia. wood pole	pole (optional)
1	1⅜-inch-dia.	wooden closet pole socket	pole (optional)
1 box	1¾-inch	galvanized finish nails	
1 box	1-inch	galvanized finish nails	
1	1¼-inch	#6 brass screw	door
1	2¼-inch	#8 brass screw	hanger
1 tube		PL-200 construction adhesive	roof joints

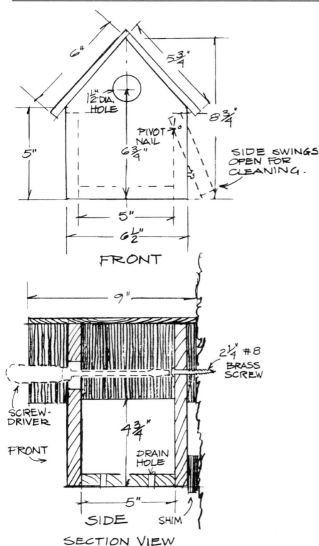

Allow about one acre of property for each bluebird house. Install the house in early spring before the birds have arrived for summer. After the birds leave in the fall, clean out (wearing gloves) any nesting material, dirt or broken eggs.

The front, back, sides and bottom pieces of the birdhouse can all be cut from one 36-inch-long 1x8. Referring to the Cutting Plan (see Fig. 1), measure and mark the dimensions for the front and back pieces, each measuring 6½ inches wide by 8¾ inches long. Clamp the lumber to your work table, and using a handsaw or an electric jigsaw (see p. 27, Fig. 30), cut off these two pieces. Draw a vertical line down the center of both pieces, then measure 5 inches up from each bottom corner and make a mark. Connect the two side marks to the top of the center line, forming a peak (see Fig. 2). Reclamp the wood to the workbench and cut along these lines to make the gabled front and back pieces of the house. **NOTE:** The decorative leaf carving on the front of the birdhouse is optional, but if you want to include it, this is the time to do the carving. Directions are given at the end of the project.

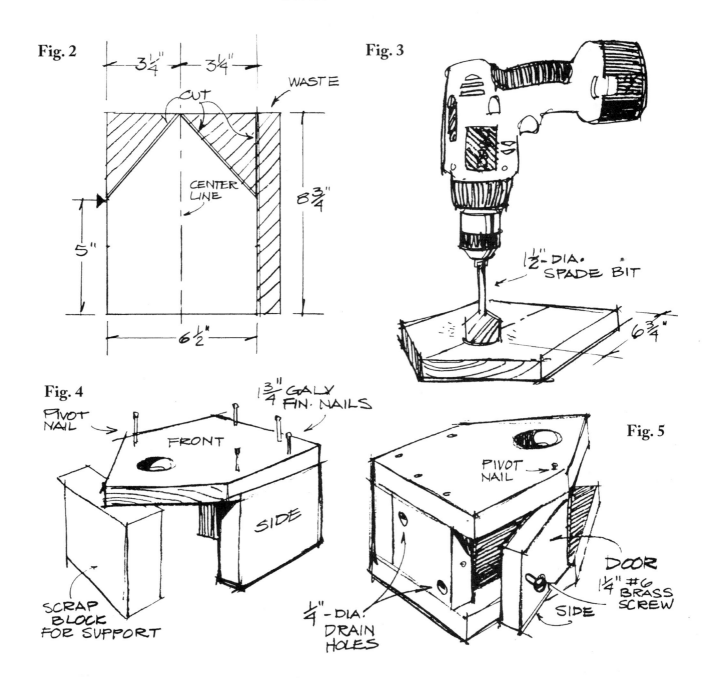

Fig. 2

Fig. 3

Fig. 4

Fig. 5

Again referring to the Cutting Plan (see Fig. 1), measure, mark and cut the two side pieces, each measuring 4¾ inches long by 5 inches wide, and then the bottom piece, measuring 5 inches square. **TIP:** Clamp the wood to your work surface *each time* you make a cut.

Use a 1½-inch spade bit to carefully drill a 1½-inch-diameter entrance hole through the center line of the front piece, 6¾ inches up from the bottom (see Fig. 3). (For mountain and western

bluebirds, make the hole 1⁹⁄₁₆ inches in diameter.) Then drill two ¼-inch-diameter holes in the bottom piece to function as drain holes, in case rain blows in.

Nail the front piece to the bottom and to the left side piece, using four 1¾-inch galvanized finish nails spaced 1 inch apart. Place a piece of scrap wood or a brick to support the front piece of wood while you are nailing (see Fig. 4). Turn the unit over and do the same for the back piece.

Attach the right side piece (the door) last, nailing one 1¾-inch finish nail through the upper corner of the front and another 1¾-inch finish nail through the upper corner of the back, then into the edges of the side piece (see Figs. 4 and 5). These two nails serve as pivots, so that the right side of the birdhouse can swing open for cleaning. Keep it closed the rest of the year by screwing a 1¼-inch #6 galvanized or brass screw through the side and into the base of the house. This can easily be unscrewed for a yearly spring cleaning.

For the roof, cut two 9-inch-wide cedar shingles to measure 5¾ inches long; the remaining two measure 6 inches long. Use 1-inch galvanized finish nails, spaced approximately 1½ inches apart, to attach the shingles to the top edges of the front and back of the house (see Fig. 6). Overlap the 5¾-inch-long shingle with the 6-inch-long one where they join at the peak of the roof, to prevent rain from seeping in. Use PL-200 construction adhesive to hold the joints together at the top, since the wood there is too thin for nails.

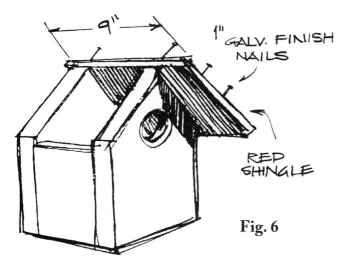

Fig. 6

NOTE: Single shingles can often be found loose where the shingles are sold at the lumberyard. If they are not available in your area, you can substitute a scrap of ½-inch rough exterior plywood for the roofing material.

Install the bluebird house 4 to 6 feet above the ground, either on a post or a tree, with the entrance hole facing away from the prevailing wind. For a post, use an 8-foot-long 1⅜-inch-diameter pole and soak the bottom in preservative before burying it 2 feet deep in the ground. A 1⅜-inch wooden closet pole socket makes an easy attachment for the birdhouse on top of the pole.

If you are attaching the birdhouse to a tree, use a ⅛-inch drill bit to drill a hole in the back of the house, opposite the bird's front entrance hole. Open the side door and insert the 2¼-inch brass screw through the back hole, while holding the house in place with the other hand. Insert a screwdriver through the front hole and into the screw in the back hole, screwing the birdhouse onto the tree (see p. 121, Side Section View).

Avoid the temptation of setting a perch outside the entrance hole, as this could make it easier for a squirrel to take ownership and move in.

DECORATIVE CARVING
(OPTIONAL):

An easy way to carve out a graceful leaf decoration on the front of the birdhouse is with a ½-inch #7 shallow wood gouge. Practice on scrap wood first until you feel confident about holding the tool and shaping the design that you have drawn. **TIP:** It's easier to draw and cut your leaf design on the front piece of the birdhouse before putting the house together.

Draw your design on the front piece with a pencil (see Fig. 7), then use a utility knife to cut out the vine part, making two slanted cuts that meet, forming a "V" (see Fig. 8). Cut out the leaves with the gouge, incising the wood approximately ⅛ inch deep. Position the chisel at a slight

Fig. 7

Fig. 8

$\frac{1}{2}$" GOUGE #7 SWEEP →

Fig. 9

Fig. 10

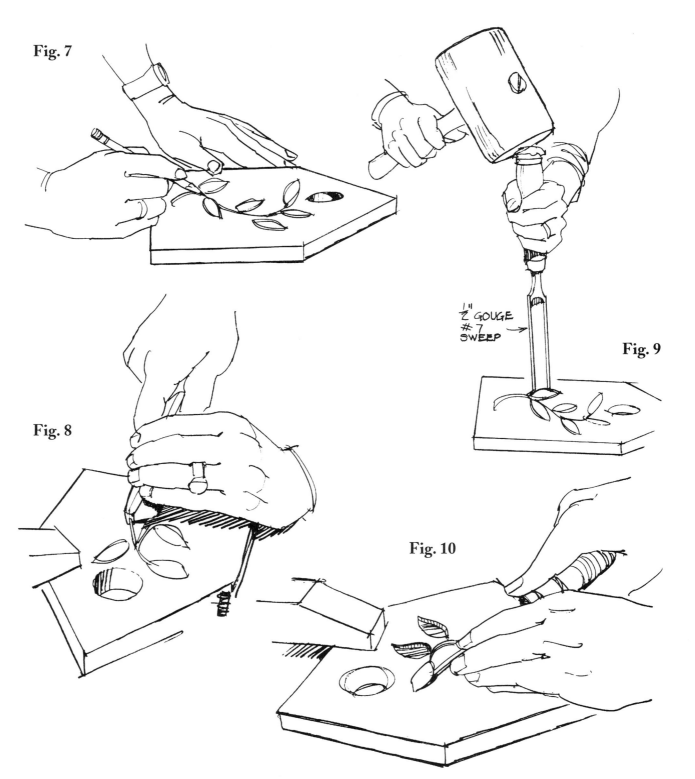

angle on the outline of the leaf, and tap gently with a wood mallet on the gouge handle (see Fig. 9). Each leaf will require approximately two cuts to form each side of a leaf. Clean out the excess wood in the center of each leaf with a ¼-inch straight chisel. Hold the chisel tightly against the

wood, using one hand to guide the tool and the other to push it against the wood (see Fig. 10). Don't worry about making your cuts so that they conform exactly to what you have drawn. Let them be free-form, reflecting a design unique to your birdhouse.

Bird

FEEDER

EVERY BIRDHOUSE deserves a bird feeder nearby, especially one that can be seen from the dining room or kitchen windows. It should be located in a place that is easily accessible for replenishing birdseed but not within reach of squirrels and more aggressive birds like blue jays. This bird feeder, designed for finches, wrens and other small birds, is accessible from two sides, so the birds won't be trapped if an enemy appears.

The ledges and sides for the feeder are cut from an 11-inch piece of 1x6 cedar (see Cutting Plan, Fig. 1). Begin by rip-cutting the two ledge pieces. Clamp the board to your workbench so that the long side of the board overlaps the bench by 1½ inches (see Fig. 2). Measure and mark a line, 1 inch in from and parallel to the long side

of the board. Using a handsaw or electric jigsaw, rip-cut along the pencil line. **NOTE:** Be sure to cut on the waste side of the line, leaving a 4½-inch-wide piece of wood in the clamp. By cutting on the waste side of the line, you will end up with a piece of wood for the ledge that is a little less than 1 inch wide.

Measure, mark and cut the ripped piece of wood into two 4-inch-long pieces. These will be used for the ledges of the bird feeder.

Draw a vertical line down the center of the remaining 4½x11-inch board. Measure and mark 2 inches down from each corner of the board (see Fig. 3). Draw a diagonal line from the 2-inch mark on both sides to the center line as shown. Clamp the board to your workbench and cut off both corners. Turn the board around, reposition the clamp and repeat the same procedure on the opposite end of the board.

MATERIALS LIST

Quantity	Size	Description	Location or Use
2	5½x4½ inches	1x6 #2 common cedar	sides
2	1x4 inches	1x6 #2 common cedar	ledges
1	5½x4½ inches	¼-inch exterior plywood	bottom
1	4 inches	1x2 #2 common pine	ridgepole
2	6x4 inches	red cedar shingles	roof
1 box	1-inch	galvanized wire nails	
1 box	1½-inch	galvanized finish nails	
1 bottle	8 oz.	Titebond II glue	
2	¾-inch	screw eyes	hangers
2 yards		nylon string	
1 sheet	9x11 inches	60-grit sandpaper	

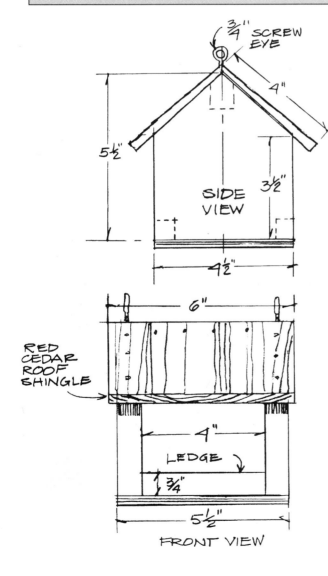

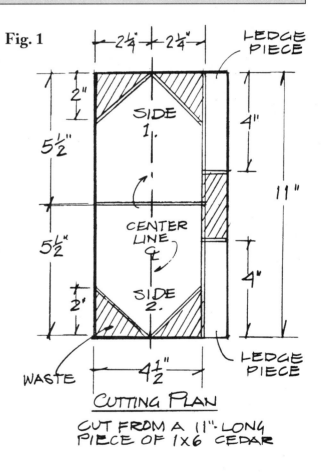

Fig. 1

CUTTING PLAN

CUT FROM A 11"-LONG PIECE OF 1x6 CEDAR

After the four diagonal corners have been sawed off, measure 5½ inches down from one end of the board. Make a mark and draw a straight

Fig. 2

RIP-CUT 1"
OFF THE 1X6
FOR THE LEDGES.

1"

1½

Fig. 4

BACKUP
SUPPORT

GLUE &
NAIL

USE A SOLID BACKUP
PIECE TO REST REST
THE PIECES AGAINST WHILE
YOU ARE NAILING THE BOTTOM
ONTO THE SIDES.

CUT OFF
CORNERS

4½"

5½"

2¼"

2"

Fig. 3

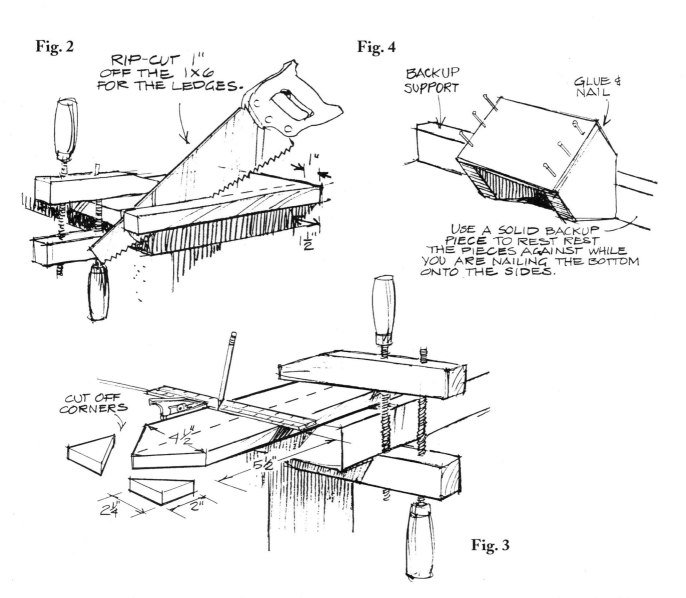

line across the board at this point (see Fig. 3). Cut the board in half, creating two identical side pieces each 5½ inches long. Hold the two pieces flush together; if they are not exactly the same size, use a rasp or 60-grit sandpaper and a sanding block (see p. 53-54 and Figs. 78 and 79) to make them equal.

From a piece of ¼-inch exterior plywood, measure, mark and cut the 5½x4½-inch bottom piece for the bird feeder, using a handsaw or electric jigsaw (see p. 27, Fig. 30). To attach the bottom piece to the side pieces, squeeze a bead of Titebond II glue over the bottom edges of the sides pieces, spreading it evenly with a flat stick.

Place the bottom piece over the ends of the side pieces, and hammer 1-inch galvanized wire nails every 1 inch, through the bottom piece and into the bottom edges of the two side pieces (see Fig. 4).

Squeeze a bead of glue along one side of the two 4-inch-long ledge pieces, spreading it evenly. Place them, glued-side down, between the two side pieces, aligning them so all edges are flush. Using 1-inch galvanized wire nails, equally spaced, hammer through the bottom piece and into the ledge pieces. **NOTE:** Use the corner of your workbench as a support while you are nailing (see Fig. 5).

Fig. 5

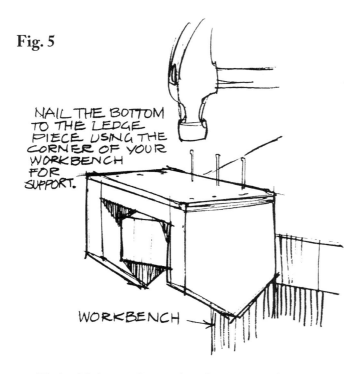

NAIL THE BOTTOM TO THE LEDGE PIECE USING THE CORNER OF YOUR WORKBENCH FOR SUPPORT.

WORKBENCH

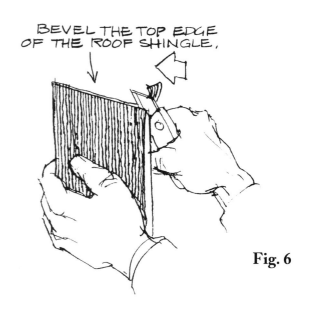

BEVEL THE TOP EDGE OF THE ROOF SHINGLE.

Fig. 6

To build the roof, use a handsaw or an electric jigsaw to cut two pieces of red cedar shingles, 6 inches wide by 4 inches tall. Using a utility knife with a sharp new blade, bevel the top edges of the two shingles so they will fit together neatly at the peak of the roof (see Fig. 6). **NOTE:** Always cut away from yourself.

Sand the bevel with 60-grit sandpaper and a sanding block and check to make sure the shingles join together perfectly.

To make the ridgepole, cut a piece of 1x2 to fit the 4-inch inside dimension between the two sides at the roof. Draw a line across the middle of the top edge of the ridgepole and use a utility knife to bevel the top edges to the same angle as the peak of the roof (see Fig. 7). Apply glue to the ends of the ridgepole and place it between the side

pieces at the top. Hammer two 1½-inch finish nails, 1 inch apart, through the sides and into the ridgepole (see Fig. 8).

Position the two shingles over the ridgepole, allowing them to overlap the sides of the bird feeder by ¼ inch. Glue the top edges of the shingles together. Using 1-inch galvanized wire nails, nail the shingles to the ridgepole and to the sides of the bird feeder, placing the nails approximately 1 inch apart (see p. 126, Front View). Screw a ¾-inch screw eye to either end of the peak of the roof (see p. 126, Side and Front Views), and hang the feeder to a tree limb that you can see from your window.

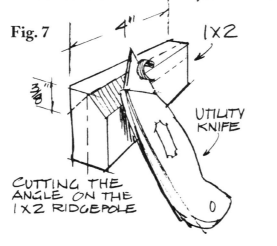

Fig. 7

4"

3/8"

1X2

UTILITY KNIFE

CUTTING THE ANGLE ON THE 1X2 RIDGEPOLE

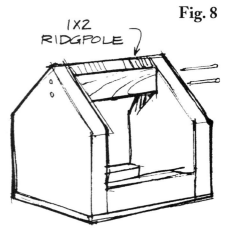

Fig. 8

1X2 RIDGPOLE

Headboard

WITH STORAGE

THIS HEADBOARD serves two purposes—it provides a slanted support for your head and back while reading or watching television in bed, and it contains a two-part storage area for blankets, sheets and pillows. One storage area is underneath the false bottom; the other is above it. Storage is easily accessible by flipping the hinged front panel open from the top. Our plans are for one front panel; however, you also can make the headboard with two front panels, as pictured on p. 40.

Before beginning this project, measure the height and width of the bed that you will be using. These plans are for a 20-inch-high by 54-inch-wide double bed. If your bed differs in size, you will need to adjust these measurements.

Begin by cutting out the pieces from the 4x8-foot sheet of ¾-inch birch plywood. Lay the plywood on top of two sawhorses and, referring to the Cutting Plan (see Fig. 1), use a tape measure and T-square, or a straightedge, to measure and mark the cut lines for the headboard pieces. Cut out the pieces using a portable circular saw (see p. 26, Fig. 28B) and a straightedge as your guide. To easily identify the pieces once you begin assembling them, it's helpful to lightly label each one in pencil.

Next, cut the pieces for the back and false bottom. Both the 28½x55½-inch back and the 8¾x53¾-inch false bottom can be cut from one 4x8-foot sheet of ¼-inch exterior plywood, following the same procedure described above.

MATERIALS LIST

Quantity	Size	Description	Location or Use
1	15½x54 inches	¾-inch birch plywood	front
2	9¾x28½ inches	¾-inch birch plywood	sides
1	5½x54 inches	¾-inch birch plywood	top
1	9x54 inches	¾-inch birch plywood	bottom
1	14½x54 inches	¾-inch birch plywood	door
1	28½x55½ inches	¼-inch exterior plywood	back
1	8¾x53¾ inches	¼-inch exterior plywood	false bottom
2	54 inches	1x6 #2 common pine	base
2	7½ inches	1x6 #2 common pine	base
2	54 inches	1x2 #2 common pine	supports
2	7½ inches	1x2 #2 common pine	supports
1 box	2½-inch	galvanized finish nails	
1 box	1⅝-inch	white annular panel nails	
1 bottle	8 oz.	carpenter's glue	
1	54 inches	1½-inch continuous (piano) hinge	
1 sheet	9x11 inches	120-grit sandpaper	
1 roll	¾-inch	birch edge-banding tape	
1 can	quart	clear wood sealer or paint	

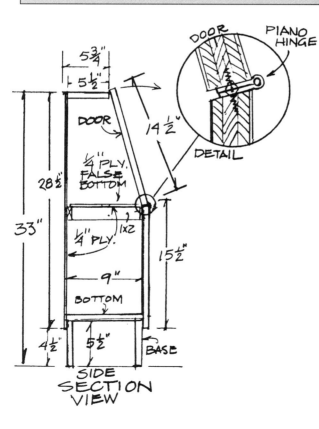

SIDE SECTION VIEW

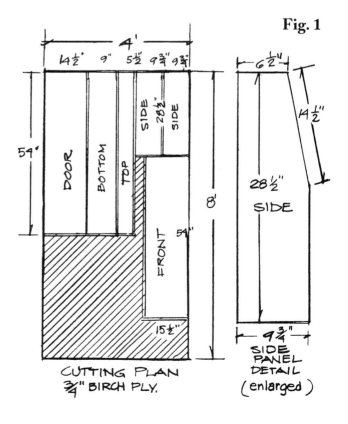

Fig. 1

CUTTING PLAN ¾" BIRCH PLY.

SIDE PANEL DETAIL (enlarged)

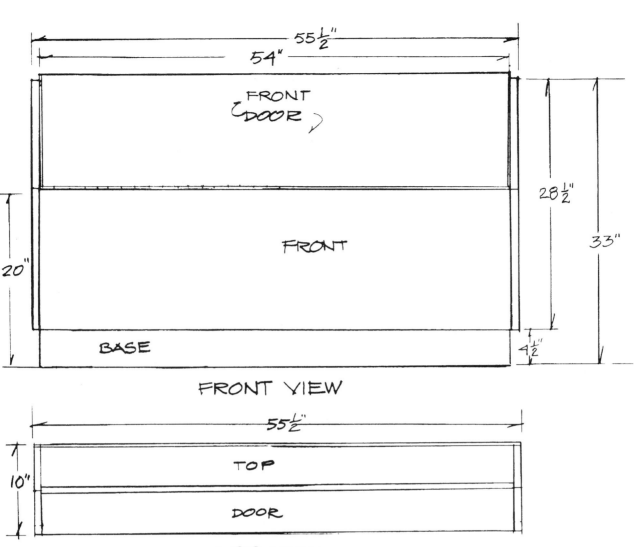

55½"

54"

FRONT DOOR

FRONT

28½"

33"

20"

BASE

4½"

FRONT VIEW

55½"

TOP

10"

DOOR

TOP VIEW

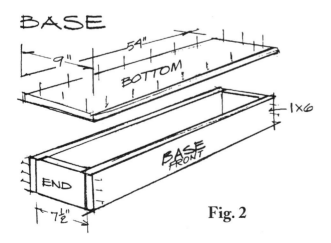

BASE

54"

9"

BOTTOM

1x6

BASE FRONT

END

7½"

Fig. 2

To make the base for the headboard, lay a 12-foot piece of 1x6 #2 pine on top of two sawhorses.

Measure and use a speed square (see p. 30, Fig. 37) to mark a cut line at 7½ inches. Cut the board off using a portable circular saw. Repeat this procedure to make a second identical 7½-inch-long end piece. Measure, mark and cut two more base pieces, each 54 inches long. Using three 2½-inch galvanized finish nails, nail the two 54-inch-long front and back base pieces to the two 7½-inch-long end base pieces, so that the front and back pieces overlap the edges of the end pieces (see Fig. 2). Lay the 9x54-inch bottom piece over the base unit and nail it to the base, placing the nails 6 inches apart and ⅜ inch from the edge on each side.

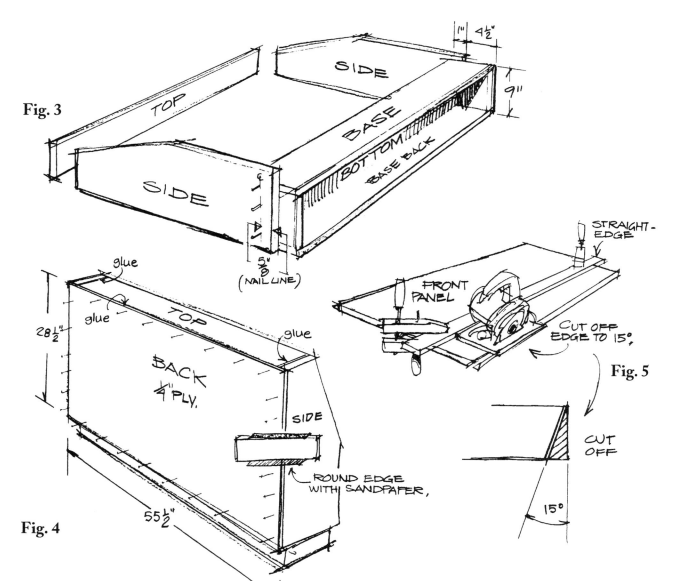

Fig. 3

1" 4½"

9"

TOP

SIDE

BASE

SIDE

BOTTOM

BASE BACK

⅝"
(NAIL LINE)

glue

glue

glue

28½"

TOP

BACK
¼" PLY.

SIDE

ROUND EDGE
WITH SANDPAPER.

55½"

Fig. 4

STRAIGHT-
EDGE

FRONT
PANEL

CUT OFF
EDGE TO 15°

Fig. 5

CUT
OFF

15°

For the side panels, measure 6½ inches in from one end of each side panel and draw a line from this point 14½ inches down to the side edge of each panel (see Side Panel Detail, Fig. 1). Clamp a straightedge to the side panel and use it as a guide to make a perfectly straight cut with a portable circular saw.

Turn the base unit over so it is lying on its back (see Fig. 3) and position the two side panels so they are 4½ inches above the bottom of the base. Glue and nail the side panels to the base, using 1⅝-inch white annular panel nails placed 2 inches apart, but starting them ⅝ inch in from the edges.

Squeeze a bead of carpenter's glue along the 5½-inch-long side edges of the top piece, spreading it evenly with a flat stick. Fit the top piece between the two side panels and nail the sides to the top at the edges, hammering three 1⅝-inch white annular panel nails through each side, ⅜ inch in from the edge.

Stand the unit up and glue and nail the ¼-inch plywood back piece to the back edges of the top, side panels and base, hammering 1⅝-inch white annular panel nails every 4 inches, starting them ⅜ inch in from the edges (see Fig. 4).

NOTE: To avoid seeing the exposed edge of the plywood, sand its corner edge back at a slight

Fig. 6

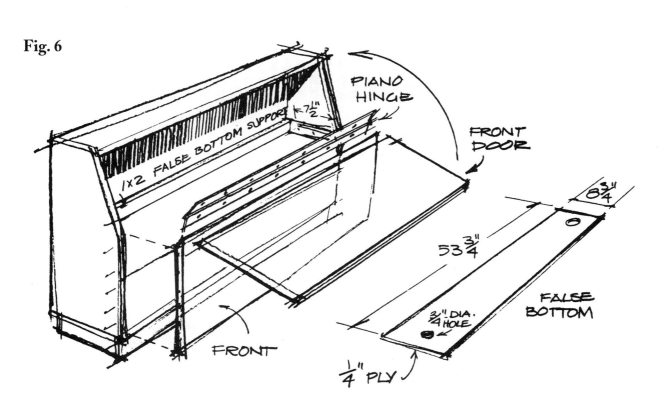

angle, using 60-grit sandpaper and a sanding block (see p. 53-54 and Figs. 78 and 79).

Turn the unit over, back side down. Before installing the front panel, use a portable circular saw to make a beveled edge to which the door will be hinged. Do this by cutting the top edge of the front piece at a 15-degree angle (see Fig. 5). Then squeeze a bead of glue along the side edges and bottom of the front panel, spreading it evenly. Put the front panel in place. Nail the side panels to the front panel, using 1⅝-inch annular panel nails spaced approximately 4 inches apart. Then nail the front panel to the bottom, spacing the annular panel nails approximately 2 inches apart.

To support the false bottom, cut two 54-inch-long 1x2 #2 pine support pieces and two 7½-inch-long 1x2 support pieces. Squeeze a bead of glue along the back side of the support pieces and fit them inside the storage compartment, ¼ inch below the top of the front (see Fig. 6).

Using a hacksaw, cut 18 inches off the 6-foot-long piano hinge, leaving you with a 54-inch hinge. Screw one leaf of the hinge to the bottom edge of the door piece and the other leaf to the top edge of the front panel, enabling the door to swing open (see Fig. 6).

Since the bottom section of the compartment can also be used for storage, the false bottom is removable. Using a ¾-inch spade bit (see p. 32, Fig. 41), drill a ¾-inch-diameter hole in each end of the ¼-inch plywood false bottom (see Fig. 6) to make finger holes, so that it can easily be lifted out, accessing the area below. Sand the holes with a rolled-up scrap of 120-grit sandpaper (see p. 83, Fig. 11).

To finish the exposed edges of the headboard, apply edge-banding tape using an ordinary household iron. Finish with a clear wood sealer or a paint of your choice.

Scandinavian
SINGLE BED

THIS SIMPLE BED, constructed from stock lumber, can be built in less than a day. The legs and frame are made of spruce, a softwood light in weight and color that lends itself to carving and is more economical than fir. The headboard and footboard are cut from a single piece of clear pine. All of the parts of the bed are screwed together, resulting in a strong yet lightweight bed. **NOTE:** Because mattresses can vary slightly in size, before starting this project be sure to measure the mattress you will be using, and make any necessary adjustments.

This bed is ideal for a guest room or child's room. We built ours for our daughter, Lief Anne, who helped us design the heart and the leaf and vine shapes. These, or your own designs, can be carved with a utility knife and a ½-inch #7 gouge (see p. 123-124, Decorative Carving). Or use a jigsaw to cut out shapes from ¼-inch plywood and glue them to the headboard. Another option is stenciling.

Carefully pick out the straightest, clearest pieces of lumber you can find at the lumberyard. Look for three 7-foot lengths of #2 spruce containing as few knots as possible. You'll need one knot-free 78½-inch length of 2x6 spruce for the side of the bed frame that will be seen the most. If both sides of the bed will be visible, choose two knot-free lengths. The remaining 7-foot 2x6 will be cut for the head frame and foot frame.

MATERIALS LIST

Quantity	Size	Description	Location or Use
2	78½ inches	2x6 #2 spruce	bed frame sides
2	39½ inches	2x6 #2 spruce	bed frame head & foot
4	32 inches	2x4 #2 spruce	legs
2	42½ inches	5/4x8 clear pine	headboard & footboard
2	75½ inches	1x2 #2 common pine	ledge
10	39½ inches	1x4 #2 common pine	mattress supports
1 box	1¼-inch	#10 Phillips-head screws	bed frame
1 box	2½-inch	#10 flathead screws	bed frame
1 bottle	8 oz.	carpenter's glue	
1 sheet	9x11 inches	60-grit sandpaper	
1 sheet	9x11 inches	120-grit sandpaper	
8	3/8-inch-dia. x ¼-inch	wood plugs	
12	½-inch-dia. x ¼-inch	wood plugs	
1 can	10 oz.	wood putty	

Refer to the Cutting Plan (see Fig. 1) as you cut out the various pieces, beginning with the bed frame. Place one 7-foot-long 2x6 on two sawhorses or other work supports. Since lumber is not always square at the end, check to make sure that your piece is. If it isn't, draw a line perpendicular to the long edge of the board, 1 inch in from the end, and cut it off, using a portable circular saw and a speed square (see p. 30, Fig. 37). Make sure that the saw blade cuts on the waste side of the line. Measure down 78½ inches from the end you just cut, draw another line perpendicular to the long edge of the board, and cut off the end of the board, again making sure that the saw blade is cutting on the waste side of the line. Repeat this procedure with the other 7-foot 2x6. You now have the two sides of the bed frame. Cut the remaining 2x6 into two shorter

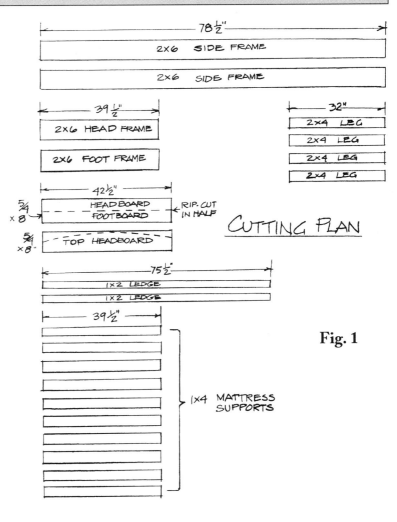

Fig. 1

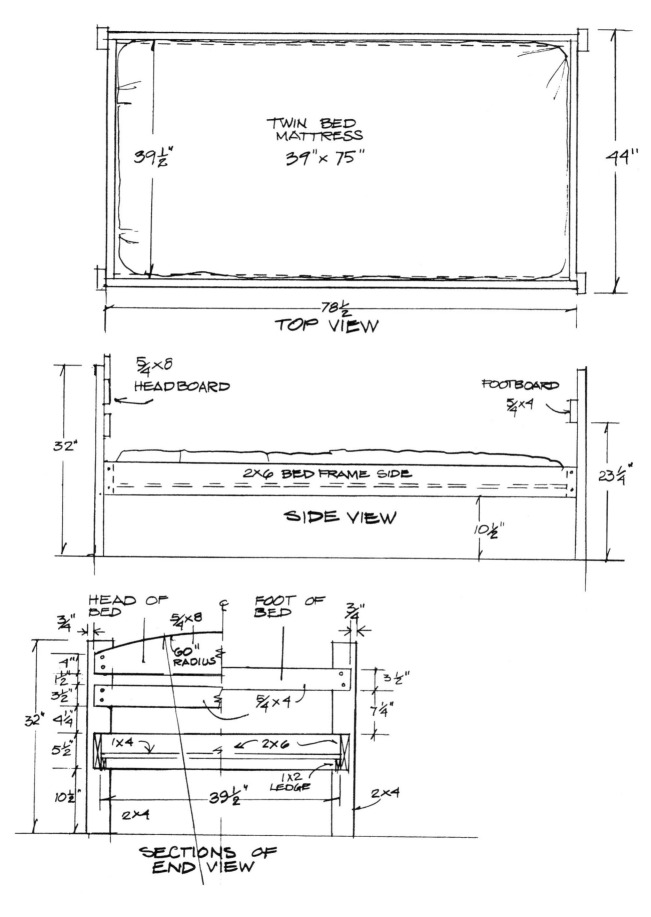

TWIN BED
MATTRESS
39" × 75"

39½"

44"

78½"

TOP VIEW

5/4×8
HEADBOARD

FOOTBOARD
5/4×4

32"

2X6 BED FRAME SIDE

23¼"

SIDE VIEW

10½"

HEAD OF
BED

FOOT OF
BED

5/4×8

60"
RADIUS

¾"

¾"

1"

1½"

3½"

4¼"

5½"

32"

10½"

1X4

5/4×4

3½"

7¼"

2X6

1X2
LEDGE

39½"

2X4

2X4

SECTIONS OF
END VIEW

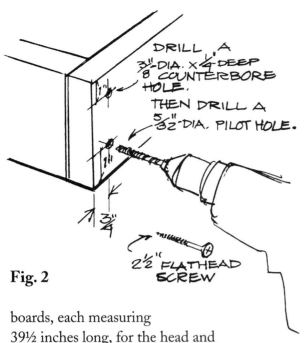

DRILL A
3/8"-DIA. X 1/4-DEEP
COUNTERBORE
HOLE.

THEN DRILL A
5/32"-DIA. PILOT HOLE.

1"

1"

3/4"

2 1/2" FLATHEAD
SCREW

Fig. 2

boards, each measuring 39½ inches long, for the head and foot frames.

To make the holes for the screws that hold the bed parts together, lay the two 78½-inch boards across your sawhorses and measure and mark two points, each ¾ inch from the ends of the boards and 1 inch from the top and bottom edges (see Fig. 2). Using a ⅜-inch spade bit (see p. 49, Fig. 70), drill two ⅜-inch-diameter holes ¼ inch deep at the marked points. Then drill two 5/32-inch pilot holes at the same points through the 2x6s.

Place your bed frame pieces in position on the floor (see Fig. 3), and using a wall or some other

stationary object as a support, screw a 2½-inch #10 flathead screw into each hole and into the ends of the 2x6 head and foot pieces (see Fig. 2). Fill the counterbored holes with either wood putty or a ⅜-inch-diameter by ¼-inch wood plug, which you can find at most hardware stores and lumberyards.

Cut the four legs, each 32 inches long, from a 12-foot 2x4, using the same method and tools as described above for the bed frame. To join the legs to the bed frame, tilt the bed frame up on its side and slide two pieces of ¾-inch-thick scrap lumber under it in order to raise it off the floor (see Fig. 4). Place a 2x4 leg against the end of the frame so that 10½ inches extend past the bottom of the frame. To mark the screw holes, measure and make a pencil mark 11½ inches up from the bottom of the leg and 2 inches in from the outside edge of the leg (see Detail, Fig. 4). Measure up an additional 3½ inches and make another mark. Then measure 1 inch from the top inside edge of the leg, equidistant from the first two holes, and make a third mark. Using a ½-inch spade bit, counterbore a ½-inch-diameter ¼-inch-deep hole at each mark. Glue and screw the legs to the bed frame, using 1¼-inch #10 Phillips-head screws. Repeat this procedure for the remaining three legs. Fill the screw holes with wood putty or ½-inch-diameter by ¼-inch wood plugs.

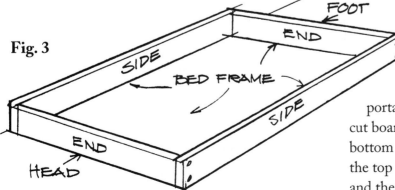

Fig. 3

FOOT
END
SIDE
BED FRAME
SIDE
END
HEAD

Referring again to the Cutting Plan (see Fig. 1), cut the pieces for the headboards and footboard. Cut two 42½-inch-long sections from an 85-inch piece of 5/4x8 clear pine. Rip-cut one of these in half, using a portable circular saw. Place one of the rip-cut boards at the head of the bed so that its bottom edge is 4¼ inches above and parallel to the top edge of the head end of the bed frame, and the board is ¾ inch in from the edge of the leg. Glue and screw the headboard to the inside of the legs, using two 1¼-inch Phillips-head screws. Do the same for the footboard, but place it so that its bottom edge is 7¼ inches above and parallel to the top edge of the foot end of the bed frame (see p. 136, Sections of End View).

To make the top part of the headboard, mark a 60-inch-radius curve in the top of the remaining piece of ⁵⁄₄x8 clear pine. This curve can be established by making a simple "beam compass," using one of the 1x2 pine ledge pieces or any 6-foot-long piece of 1x2 (see Fig. 5). Drill a ¼-inch hole near the end of the 1x2 and insert a pencil. From the center of this hole, measure 60 inches toward the other end of the 1x2 and hammer in a 2-inch nail at this point. With the pencil, mark the midpoint of the ⁵⁄₄x8. To locate the pivot point for the compass, strike an arc from a point that is 4 inches up from the bottom edge of each end of the headboard. The point at which the two arcs intersect is the pivot point for the 60-inch-radius curve. Reverse the position of the beam compass so that the pencil point rests on one of the two 4-inch points and the nail rests on the intersect point. Hold the nail steady, and draw the arc on the headboard with the beam compass. Carefully cut the curve out, using an electric jigsaw (see p. 28, Fig. 32). Sand the curve smooth, using 60-grit and 120-grit sandpaper and a sanding block (see p. 53-54 and Figs. 78 and 79).

NOTE: If you wish to carve the headboard using our heart design, lay the headboard on a flat surface and trace the heart shapes onto the wood, using our design as a guide (see p. 139, Heart Design instructions). Cut the top curves of the hearts out using a 1½-inch-diameter spade bit and cutting only ⅛ inch deep into the wood. Cut the bottom half of the hearts out using a ¼-inch chisel (see Fig. 6).

After you have finished carving out your design, glue and screw the decorative headboard to the inside of the legs so that its bottom edge is 1½ inches

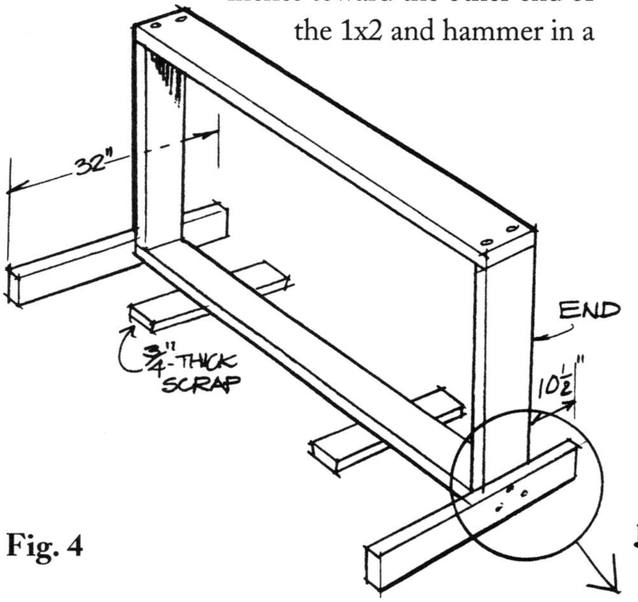

Fig. 4

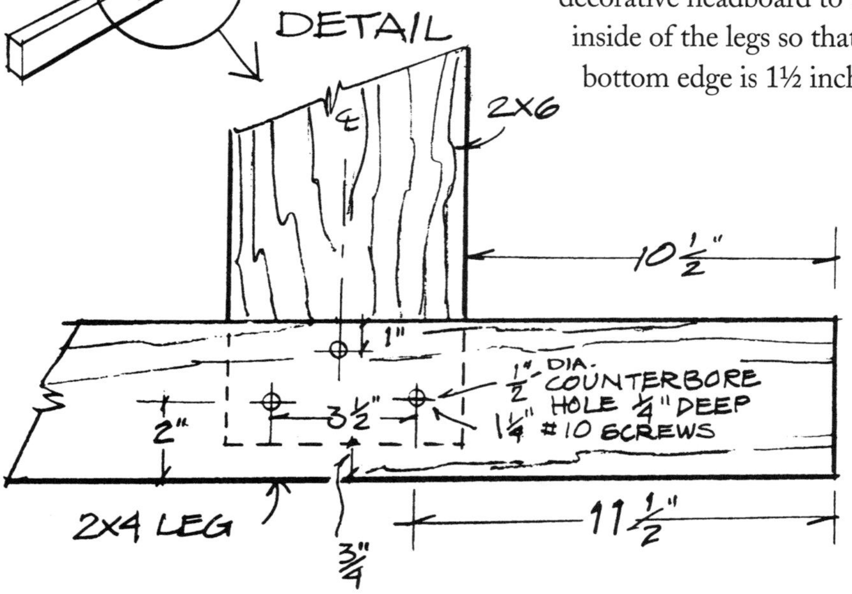

32"

¾"-THICK SCRAP

END

10½"

DETAIL

2X6

10½"

1"

1" DIA. ½" COUNTERBORE HOLE ¼" DEEP 1¼" #10 SCREWS

3½"

2"

2X4 LEG

¾"

11½"

Fig. 5

Fig. 7

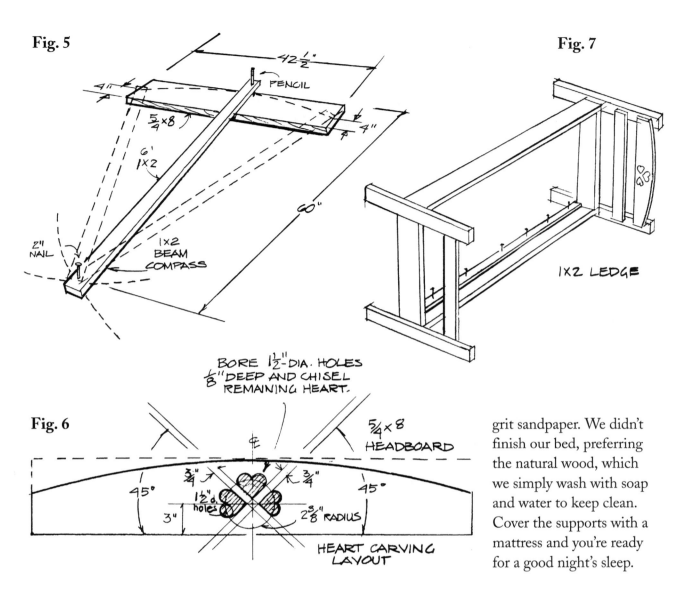

42 1/2"

PENCIL

4"

5/4 x 8

4"

6'
1x2

60"

1x2
BEAM
COMPASS

2"
NAIL

1X2 LEDGE

BORE 1 1/2"-DIA. HOLES
1/8" DEEP AND CHISEL
REMAINING HEART.

Fig. 6

5/4 x 8
HEADBOARD

¢

45°

3/4"

3/4"

45°

1 1/2" d.
holes

3"

2 3/8" RADIUS

HEART CARVING
LAYOUT

above and parallel to the top of the lower head-board piece (see p. 136, Sections of End View).

To hold the 1x4 mattress supports, make a ledge by cutting two pieces of 1x2 pine, each 75½ inches long. Glue and screw these support pieces to the bottom inside edge of both sides of the bed frame, spacing the 1¼-inch #10 Phillips-head screws every 6 inches (see Fig. 7).

Cut 10 mattress supports from the 1x4 pine, each measuring 39½ inches long. Space them equidistant apart and screw them into the 1x2 ledges. Sand all exposed surfaces with 60-grit sandpaper and a sanding block, followed by 120-

grit sandpaper. We didn't finish our bed, preferring the natural wood, which we simply wash with soap and water to keep clean. Cover the supports with a mattress and you're ready for a good night's sleep.

HEART DESIGN

1. Find the midpoint of the headboard and draw a vertical line.

2. Draw a horizontal line 3 inches up and parallel to the bottom edge of the board.

3. Where the two lines intersect, place the point of your compass and draw a 2⅜-inch-radius circle.

4. Using the 45-degree angle on a combination square, draw two 45-degree parallel lines, ¾ inch apart, on either side of the center point (see Fig. 6).

5. To trace the tops of the three hearts, draw six 1½-inch-diameter circles between the parallel lines.

Portable
LOFT BED

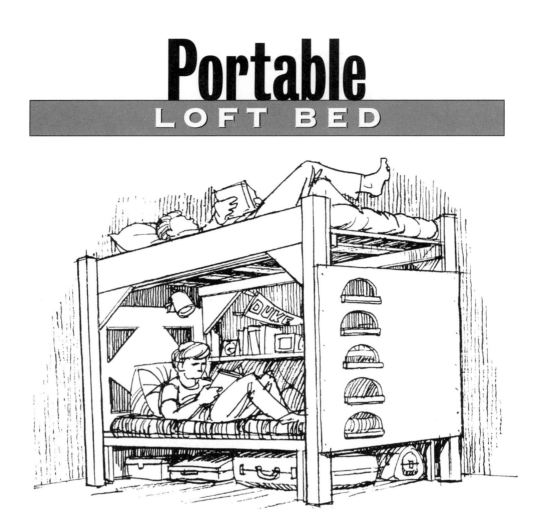

T HIS PORTABLE LOFT BED is one way
to double the space in a student's dorm
room. Putting a bed on top creates a sense
of privacy and enough room underneath for
another bed (as shown here) or a desk or couch.
This can be assembled in a couple of hours, using
only a few tools. The two rigid plywood panels
and the plywood braces give it strength, yet it is
lightweight enough to strap to a car rack. The loft
bed is completely self-supporting and requires no
holes to be drilled in the wall (another advantage
for a college dorm room).

Begin by cutting the end panels to size. Lay
two of the 4x4 posts on the ground to support the
plywood while you are cutting it. Place a 4x4-foot
¾-inch plywood panel, good side down, on the
posts and measure 3 inches in from one side,
making a mark at various points. Snap a chalk
line (see p. 30, Fig. 39) along these marks, showing where you will be cutting. Clamp a straight-
edged board to the plywood panel to act as a
guide while cutting, using an electric jigsaw or a
portable circular saw. Repeat this procedure with
the other 4x4-foot ¾-inch plywood panel. These
are the two 48x45-inch end panels (see Cutting
Plan, Fig. 1).

Next, align two of the 4x4 posts on the floor
so they are 38 inches apart. Lay one of the plywood end panels over them, so that the sides of
the panels are flush with the edges of the posts
and 10 inches from the bottom of the posts (see
Fig. 2). Use a Phillips screwdriver to screw four
2-inch #8 drywall screws equidistant apart,
through the panel and into the post on each side.

MATERIALS LIST

Quantity	Size	Description	Location or Use
2	48x45 inches	¾-inch exterior plywood	end panels
4	14x14 inches	¾-inch exterior plywood	end panel braces
2	*36½x40¼ inches	½-inch exterior plywood	mattress panel
4	6 feet	4x4 fir posts	corner posts
2	*80½ inches	2x4 #2 fir	bed support
2	*80½ inches	1x10 #2 common pine	side boards
6	*36½ inches	1x4 #2 common pine	cross supports
5	14 inches	¾-inch-groove cedar lattice	step caps
1	36x80 inches	dorm-size mattress	
1 box	2-inch	#8 drywall screws	
1 box	2½-inch	#10 Phillips-head screws	
1 bottle	8 oz.	Titebond II glue	

* If you wish to substitute a standard-size twin mattress for a dorm-size mattress, change these dimensions to: 39½x37¾ inches, 75½ inches, 75½ inches and 39½ inches respectively.

Fig. 1

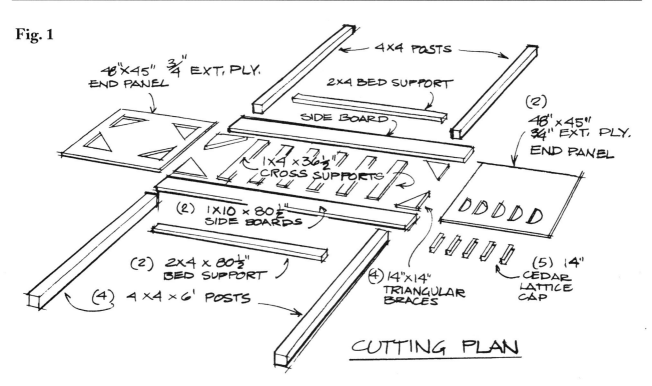

Repeat this procedure for the other end panel.

Outline the five semicircle steps on one end panel by drawing a vertical line 15 inches in from the left side and a horizontal line 9 inches down from the top of the end panel (see Fig. 3). From this point of intersection, draw a 7-inch-radius semicircle using a "pencil compass." This simple tool is made by taking a 9-inch-long stick and hammering a nail through the stick 1 inch from

Fig. 2

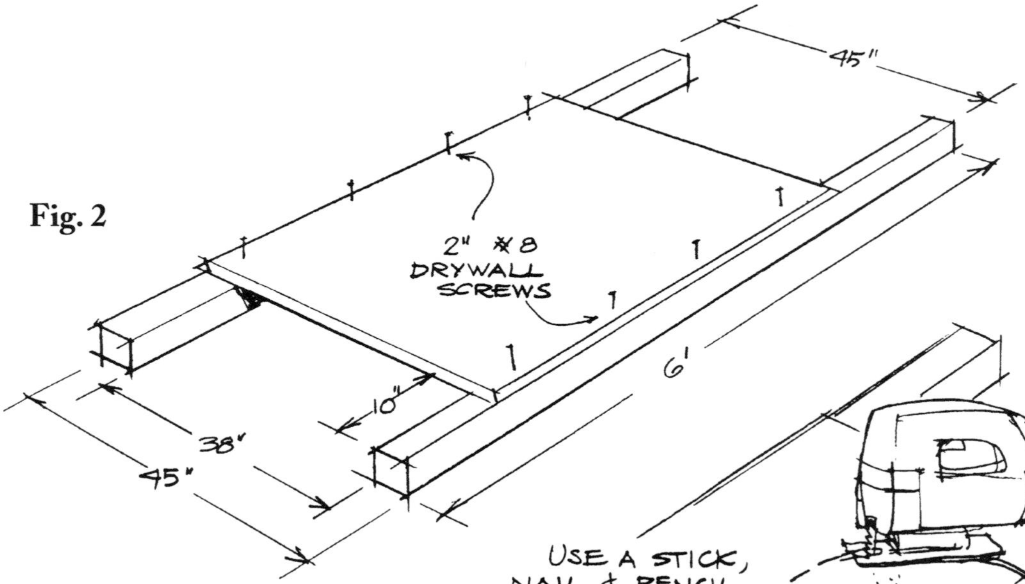

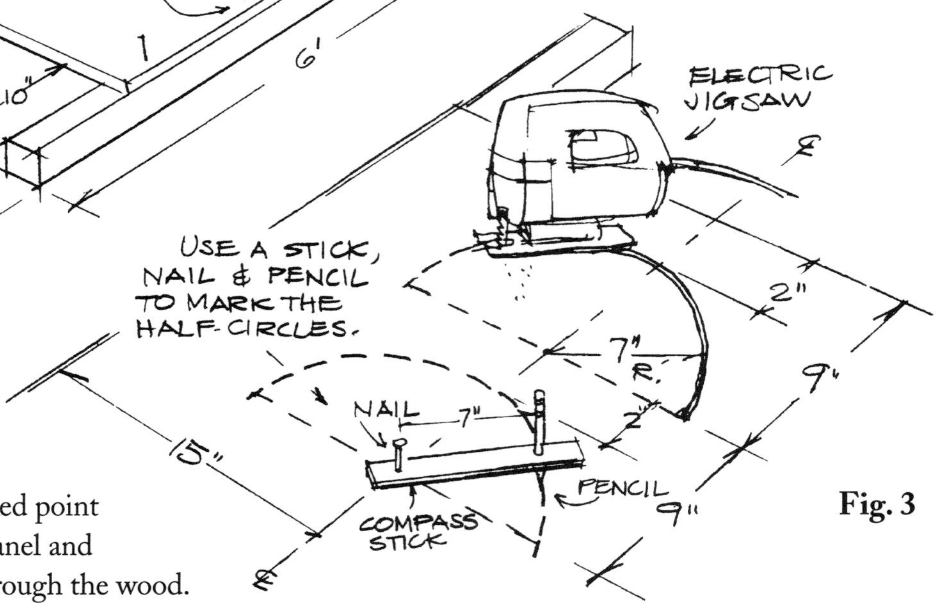

2" X 8 DRYWALL SCREWS

45"

6'

38"

45"

10"

ELECTRIC JIGSAW

USE A STICK, NAIL & PENCIL TO MARK THE HALF-CIRCLES.

NAIL 7"

COMPASS STICK

PENCIL

2"

7" R.

2"

9"

9"

15"

Fig. 3

the end. Drill a ¼-inch hole, 7 inches from the nail, and insert a pencil through the hole. Place the point of the nail at the marked point of intersection on the end panel and hammer the nail halfway through the wood. Use the pencil to scribe a semicircle to mark the cutout steps. Continue making the same measurements until you have drawn a total of five semicircles, each spaced 2 inches apart from the preceding one. **NOTE:** The bottom of each semicircle should be 9 inches below the bottom of the preceding one (see p. 143, End View).

Next, drill a ½-inch hole, starting in the corner of each semicircle and, using an electric jigsaw, cut out each semicircle. Again using an electric jigsaw, cut five 14-inch-long pieces of ¾-inch-groove cedar lattice cap. Glue them onto the top edges of the plywood steps (see Fig. 4). This makes it easier on the feet when climbing into the loft.

On the other plywood end panel, measure in 6 inches from all four sides and draw four 14-inch equilateral triangles (see p. 143, End Panel). Cut

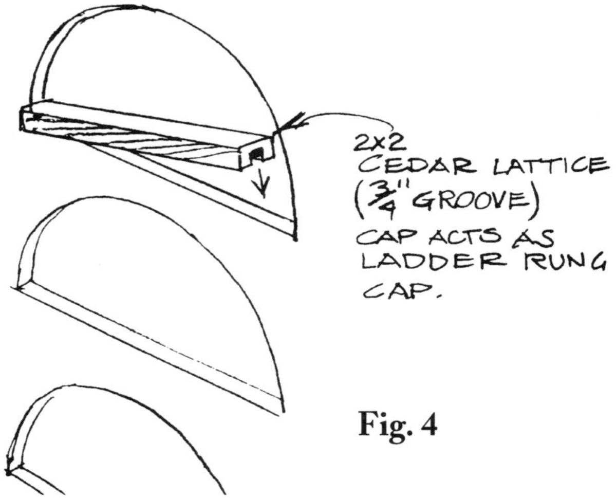

2x2 CEDAR LATTICE (¾" GROOVE) CAP ACTS AS LADDER RUNG CAP.

Fig. 4

them out with an electric jigsaw, drilling ½-inch holes at the corners to get the cuts started. (Save the cutout pieces to use as braces, but you'll need to trim off the corners with the jigsaw where the cuts were started). Screw the panel onto the remaining two posts as described earlier.

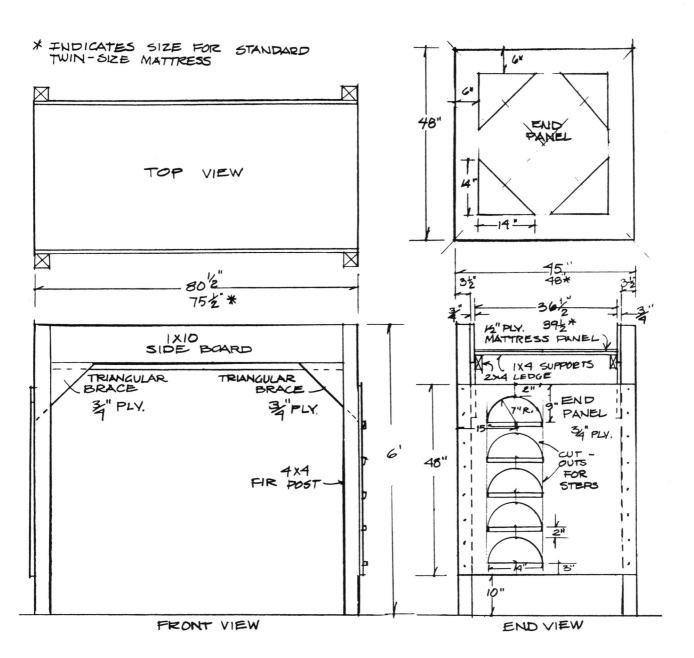

* INDICATES SIZE FOR STANDARD TWIN-SIZE MATTRESS

TOP VIEW

80½"
75½" *

1X10 SIDE BOARD

TRIANGULAR BRACE ¾" PLY.

TRIANGULAR BRACE ¾" PLY.

4X4 FIR POST

6'

FRONT VIEW

END PANEL

48"

6"
6"
4"
14"

45"
48*
3½"
3½"
¾"
¾"
36½"
½" PLY.
39½ *
MATTRESS PANEL
1X4 SUPPORTS
2X4 LEDGE

48"

2"
7" R.
15"
END PANEL ¾" PLY.
CUT-OUTS FOR STEPS
2"
4"
3"
10"

END VIEW

Referring to the Cutting Plan (see Fig. 1), cut the two 1x10s so they measure 80½ inches long. Start two 2½-inch #10 Phillips-head screws in each end of the two 1x10 side boards. Extend the screws until their points protrude through the other side. With the help of an assistant, stand the two end panels up so they are facing out (on the outside of the legs) and are 80½ inches apart. Have your helper hold one end of the first 1x10 side board up against the inside of the post so the tops of both are flush. Do the same with your end, then screw the ends of the side board to the posts (see Fig. 5). Repeat this procedure for the second side board. Once you see that they are lined up perfectly, drill a total of five 2½-inch #10 Phillips-head screws at each post's joint.

To provide a ledge for the mattress supports, use 2-inch drywall screws to fasten the two 2x4s, each 80½ inches long, to the inside of the side boards so that half of the 2x4 extends below the bottom of the side board (see Fig. 6). This also forms a lip to which the brace can be screwed. Mount the four triangular braces to the exposed

Fig. 5

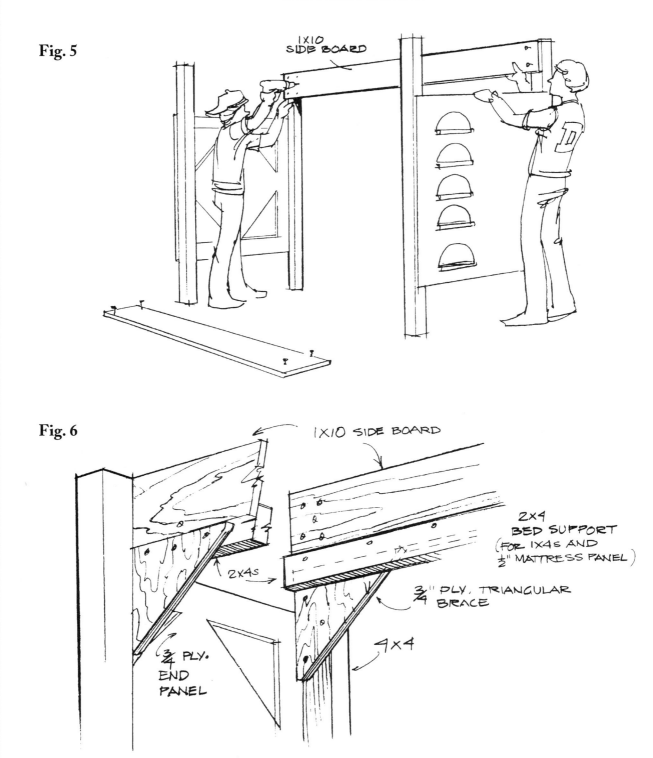

Fig. 6

surface of the 2x4s and to the inside of the 4x4 corner posts (see Fig. 6). Drill six 2-inch drywall screws through each bracket, three into the 2x4 and three into the 4x4 post.

The 2x4s also provide a ledge for the six 36½-inch-long 1x4 cross supports. Lay the cross supports equidistant from each other on top of the 2x4s and place the mattress support, made from two 4x4-foot sheets of ½-inch plywood, each cut to 36½x40¼ inches, on top of the cross supports. Finally, put the mattress on top of the plywood support. The bed is ready to be used.

Glossary of Terms

Bar clamp: A long metal bar with an adjustable clamp.

Beveled cut: An angled cut.

Board foot (as opposed to a lineal foot): A measurement of lumber that refers to all three dimensions. One board foot is 12 inches wide by 12 inches long by 1 inch thick.

Block plane: A small hand tool used to shave off or smooth lumber.

Butt hinges: Standard hinges.

Cabinet-grade plywood: Has a smooth, blemish-free face of hardwood veneer, usually birch, oak or lauan. Not suitable for outdoor exposure.

Chisel: A straight- or beveled-edged tool used for paring wood or cutting out mortises.

Combination square: A 12-inch-long measuring tool with a sliding head, which can be adjusted at different lengths. The head has one edge at a 90-degree (right) angle to the blade and the other edge at a 45-degree angle.

Counterbore: To bore a hole in order to recess a screw head. The hole is often filled with a wooden plug.

Countersink: To bore a conical hole so that a screw head can lie flush with the surface of the wood.

Crosscut: A cut running perpendicular to the grain of the wood.

Dado: A rectangular groove cut in a board.

Electric jigsaw (or saber saw): An electric portable saw used to make curved cuts.

Exterior plywood (ext. ply.): Plywood in which the plies are bonded together using exterior or waterproof glue. A structural grade of plywood used in house construction and commonly available at lumberyards. It comes in face grades of A, B and C.

Face-nailing: Nailing perpendicular to the surface of the wood.

Four-in-hand (shoe) rasp: Has rasp and file teeth on both sides.

Finish nail: A slender nail with a small cupped head, which can be driven beneath the surface of the wood with a nail set.

Framing square (or carpenter's square): A 24-inch by 16-inch L-shaped measuring tool for laying out lines. The body or long member is 2 inches wide and the tongue is 1½ inches wide. It is used to check for square on large stock.

Gouge: A chisel with a curved, hollowed blade.

Kerf: The groove made by the cut of a saw blade or the width of the cut itself.

Lag screw (or lag bolt): A large screw with a hexagonal head that is used to join heavy pieces of lumber.

Lineal foot: A measurement of lumber that refers to the length only.

Miter: An angled cut, usually 45 degrees.

Mitered cut: Used to crosscut lumber when making trim or cutting narrow pieces of stock less than 6 inches wide. A wood miter box can make 45- or 90-degree cuts.

Molding: A strip of wood with a curved surface, used for decorative purposes.

Mortise: A notch cut in a piece of wood to receive a protruding part.

Nail set: A small tool used to hammer nail heads beneath the wood's surface.

Nominal size: Size of lumber by which it is commonly known and sold (not the actual size).

Piano hinge (or continuous hinge): Extends the entire length of the two pieces of wood to be hinged together.

Phillips screwdriver bit: An attachment for an electric drill used to drive Phillips-head (cross-head) screws.

Pilot hole: A hole, slightly smaller than the nail shaft or screw thread, drilled into a piece of wood to help guide a nail or screw and to prevent splitting.

Plumb: Exactly vertical. Can be checked using a level.

Rabbet: A cut made in the edge of a board when constructing a joint.

Rasp: A rough-edged file with triangular teeth used to shape wood when a lot of material must be removed.

Rip cut: A cut made parallel to the direction of the wood grain.

Router: An electric tool used to cut grooves and shape lumber into various molding profiles.

Spade drill bit: A flat drill used for making ⅜-inch- to 1½-inch-diameter holes in wood.

Speed square: A triangular-shaped metal tool used as a guide for cutting lumber at right angles with an electric saw.

Trim: Decorative molding used to cover joints.

Twist drill bit: A durable high-speed drill used to drill small holes from 1/16 inch to 1½ inches in diameter.

Veneer: A thin sheet of wood. Veneers are glued together in layers to make plywood.

Wood clamp (or hand screw): Two wooden jaws with adjustable threaded steel rods running through them.

Wood putty: Used to fill nail holes, gaps and defects in wood.

FURTHER READING

For those who wish to delve more deeply into the intricacies
of carpentry, we recommend the following books:

Hand Tools: Their Ways and Workings, by Aldren A.
    Watson. Published by Portland House.

The author/illustrator discusses hand tools and how to use them, and includes many tips and devices to help make carpentry easier.

Reverence for Wood, by Eric Sloane. Published by Funk
    & Wagnalls.

A beautifully illustrated book describing the qualities of wood and how it was used by our American ancestors.

The Art of Japanese Joinery, by Kiyosi Seike. Published
    by Weatherhill/Tankosha.

High-end carpentry by the masters of woodworking.

Tools and How to Use Them, by Albert Jackson and
    David Day. Published by Alfred A. Knopf.

An illustrated encyclopedia of hand and power tools with more than 1,500 beautiful drawings and descriptions of how tools work.

SOURCES

TOOLS

Frog Tool Co. Ltd.
700 W. Jackson Blvd.
Chicago, IL 60661
800-648-1370

Harbor Freight Tools
3491 Mission Oaks Blvd.
Camarillo, CA 93011-6010
800-423-2567

Highland Hardware
1045 N. Highland Ave., NE
Atlanta, GA 30306
800-241-6748

The Japan Woodworker
(Chisels, gouges, files and clamps;
Catalog of fine woodworking tools)
1731 Clement Ave.
Alameda, CA 94501
800-437-7820

Klingspor's Sanding Catalogue
(Sanding machines and sandpaper)
P.O. Box 3737
Hickory, NC 28603-3737
800-228-0000

Sears Power and Hand Tools Catalog
P.O. Box 19009
Provo, UT 84605-9009
800-377-7414

Tool Traditions Catalog
(Chisels, gouges, files and clamps; Stanley tools)
7815 S. 46 St.
Phoenix, AZ 85044-5399
800-453-6736

Trend-Lines
(Sanding machines and sandpaper)
135 American Legion Hwy.
Revere, MA 02151
800-767-9999

Woodworker's Supply
1108 N. Glenn Rd.
Casper, WY 82601
800-645-9292

Woodworking
(Chisels, gouges, files and clamps;
Garrett Wade tool catalog)
161 Ave. of the Americas
New York, NY 10013
800-221-2942

HARDWARE & GLUES:

McFeely's
(Square drive screws and more)
1620 Wythe Rd., P.O. Box 3
Lynchburg, VA 24505-0003
800-443-7937

The Woodworkers' Store
21801 Industrial Blvd.
Rogers, MN 55374-9514
800-279-4441

INDEX

ABOUT THE AUTHORS

RICHARD D'ALONZO

DAVID STILES is a designer/builder and illustrator, and the author
of eight other how-to books, including *Sheds* and *The Treehouse Book*
(which won the ALA Notable Children's Book Award). A graduate of
Pratt Institute and The Academy of Fine Arts in Florence, Italy, he is
the winner of two awards from the New York Planning Commission.
His articles have appeared in *House Beautiful*, *Country Journal*,
HomeMechanix and the *New York Times*.

JEAN TRUSTY STILES, a graduate of Wheaton College, lives in
New York City, where she is an actress/model and an instructor of
English as a Second Language at Baruch College. Jeanie and David
have written *Playhouses You Can Build*, *Kid's Furniture You Can Build*
and *Garden Projects*, and have appeared on numerous television
programs, including the "Our Home" show. They have a 21-year-old
daughter, Lief-Anne, who is a student at Duke University, and divide
their time between New York City and East Hampton, New York.